adverb
verb
adjective

GRAMMAR FOR KEY STAGE 3

Angela Burt

Stanley Thornes (Publishers) Ltd

First published in 1998 by:
Stanley Thornes (Publishers) Ltd
Ellenborough House
Wellington Street
CHELTENHAM GL50 1YW
England

98 99 00 01 02 / 10 9 8 7 6 5 4 3 2 1

A catalogue record for this book is available from the British Library.

ISBN 0 7487 3367 1

Layout and typeset by D&J Hunter
Illustrated by Harry Venning
Edited by Stephanie Richards
Printed and bound in Spain by Mateu Cromo

Contents

Introduction

I believe there is a need in Years 7, 8 and 9 for a language text that deals clearly with grammatical terminology and that gives guidance on language issues in an enjoyable and practical way.

I am very much aware that lower secondary pupils now face specific grammar questions in Key Stage 3 tests and I have borne their needs in mind in writing this resource book. I have necessarily gone further and set language study in the wider context of effective communication where I believe it belongs. I want to build on and extend the skills and insights into language that pupils have gained at primary school and I want to help them exercise increasing control in their use of language.

Language in action and the range of purposes for which we make use of language are exemplified throughout the text. Examples and exercises are contextualised wherever possible and draw on a wide range of literary and non-literary sources.

Full-colour information pages are followed by photocopiable black-and-white activity sheets. I am grateful to Harry Venning for his lively line drawings and cartoons, which reinforce so well the points I have wanted to make.

The text is divided into three sections. Section One deals with words and their function within the sentence. Section Two deals with sentence structure and shows how sentences can be constructed more effectively and how common errors can be avoided. Section Three deals with paragraph structure and sequencing, essay planning, drafting and revising, and writing for different audiences and purposes in a range of genres.

In each section, pupils' attention is directed to areas where they can improve their skills with a little care. Pupils are encouraged to assess the appropriateness of language for its purpose and the impact it will have on its audience. They are invited to examine, for example, the effect achieved by switching from passive constructions to active ones and by recasting direct speech as indirect. The focus throughout is on language in action.

Since punctuation has a grammatical base, capital letters, full stops, commas, semi-colons, apostrophes and inverted commas are dealt with as they become relevant. Lists of commonly misspelt nouns, adjectives, verbs and adverbs are introduced in those subsections. Proofreading activities occur at intervals throughout the text as valuable recapitulation exercises.

Grammar need not be dull, and I hope this text will be fun to use as well as being instructive.

Angela Burt

Acknowledgements

The author and publishers are grateful to the following for permission to reproduce previously published material:

HMSO, for extract from *Hansard*, p.63. Parliamentary copyright is reproduced with the permission of the Controller of Her Majesty's Stationery Office.

HMSO, for extracts from *Tax Return Guide* and *Tax Calculation Guide*, p.86. Crown copyright is reproduced with the permission of the Controller of Her Majesty's Stationery Office.

The Office for National Statistics, for extract from marriage certificate, p.83. Crown copyright is reproduced with the permission of the Controller of Her Majesty's Stationery Office.

The Star, Dublin, for 'Spice Crisis', p.77.

Tidy Northern Ireland, for 'Litter and the Law', p.75.

The Times Educational Supplement © Times Supplements Ltd, 1998, for 'The hell of Godstone village', p.69.

© D C Thomson & Co Ltd, for advertisement from *The Beano*, p.75.

Western People, Ballina, Ireland, for 'Selling your home', p.64.

Every effort has been made to contact copyright holders and we apologise if anyone has been omitted from these acknowledgements.

The extracts quoted in exercise 96 on p.84 are taken from the following sources:
a) 'Child's Play for Mary' by Kathryn Rogers in *The Star*, Dublin, 12 November 1997.
b) Extract from advertisement, Book Tokens, November 1997.
c) *Practical Gardening Encyclopaedia*, editors Roy Hart and Roger Davies (Ward Lock 1977).
d) *Lady With A Lamp* by Cyril Davey (Lutterworth Press 1956).
e) *PCW 9512+ User Guide* (Amstrad).

Nouns

Identification

> Nouns are naming words.

Common nouns name people and things in a *general* way.

baby	pop-star	apple	chair

Proper nouns name people and places, days of the week and months of the year, and so on, *individually*. They always begin with a capital letter for this reason.

Charlotte	Liam Gallagher	Monday	Mexico

Collective nouns name collections and groups.

swarm	congregation	bouquet

Abstract nouns name ideas, feelings and states of mind.

joy	fear	pain	freedom

Gender

In English (but not in all languages!) the **gender** of nouns is quite logical.

Neuter (refers to things)

| table | chair | computer | telephone |

Masculine (refers to the male sex)

| man | boy | king | peacock |

Feminine (refers to the female sex)

| woman | girl | queen | peahen |

Common (includes both sexes)

| baby | pupil | doctor | politician |

You can avoid being sexist by using terms common to both senses:

firefighter (rather than fireman)

supervisor (rather than foreman)

head teacher (rather than headmaster/headmistress)

stable hand (rather than stable lad/stable girl)

The masculine form of a number of -ess words now includes both men and women:

poet (not poet (masculine) and poetess (feminine))

deacon (not deacon (masculine) and deaconess (feminine))

actor (not actor (masculine) and actress (feminine))

Activities

1 With a partner, look around the classroom. Write down the names of ten things that you can see beginning with **C**. (All these nouns will be common nouns.)

_____   _____   _____

_____   _____   _____

_____   _____

_____   _____

2 Supply an answer beginning with **S** to each of these questions.
(All these answers will be proper nouns and begin with a capital letter.)

a) name of a country   _____

b) name of a mountain   _____

c) name of a river   _____

d) name of a city   _____

e) surname of an author   _____

3 In small groups, identify and underline the odd one out in each of these lists.
Explain your reasoning.

a) wall   watch   window   William   web   _____

b) parent   baby   teenager   sister   child   _____

c) sadness   fear   hunger   misery   happy   _____

d) flock   crowd   audience   congregation   choir   _____

e) cub   calf   drake   lamb   foal   _____

4 Use an etymological dictionary (one that tells you about the derivation of words) to find out the countries from which we get these nouns.

a) bungalow   _____

b) sofa   _____   d) garage   _____

c) kindergarten   _____   e) yoghurt   _____

5 Suggest non-sexist terms that could replace each of the words below. You might like to work in small groups and discuss in addition whether it is worth finding non-sexist alternatives.

a) salesman   _____

b) usherette   _____

c) male nurse   _____

d) cleaning lady   _____

e) air hostess   _____

6 Replace the **bold** words in each sentence with a noun beginning with the given letter. (Notice how carefully chosen nouns can help you express yourself concisely.)

a) I will tell you **what I have decided** as soon as possible.

I will tell you my d _ _ _ _ _ _ _ as soon as possible.

b) They welcomed his **statement that he was sorry for what he had done**.

They welcomed his a _ _ _ _ _ _ .

c) The rumour that **the Queen had been arrested** spread like wildfire.

The rumour of the Queen's a _ _ _ _ _ spread like wildfire.

d) His parents do not know **what he intends to do but he has clearly made up his mind**.

His parents do not know his i _ _ _ _ _ _ _ _ _ .

e) You will have to warn her about **being late so often**.

You will have to warn her about her un _ _ _ _ _ _ _ _ _ _ _ .

7 Mrs Malaprop is a character in *The Rivals* famous for using a wrong word that sounds nearly right in place of the one needed. Circle the five malapropisms below (this kind of confusion has been named after her) and write the correct nouns in the spaces on the right.

Megan's December retort was really dreadful. _____

She made two New Year revolutions and _____

wrote them down in her new dairy. She _____

vowed to hand every homework assignation _____

in on time and to try to be a better parson. _____

That was two weeks ago. The new term had not yet begun. _____

8 Learn how to spell these twenty troublesome spellings (all nouns) for a test in a few pages' time.

a) address   h) description   o) opinion
b) advertisement i) exercise   p) opportunity
c) apology   j) families   q) parents
d) business   k) front   r) safety
e) career   l) intentions   s) sentence
f) character   m) luxury   t) speech
g) college   n) moment

Plurals

Most nouns simply add **- s** or **-e s** to form the plural

table ➡ tables

cat ➡ cats

fox ➡ fox**es**

But some groups of nouns need extra care.

Nouns ending in -y

Nouns ending in a vowel + y (-ay,-ey, -oy, -uy) are straightforward.
Add **-s.**

monkey ➡ monkeys

Nouns ending in a consonant + y (-by, -py, -ty, etc.) are more complicated.

Change **-y** to **-ies**.

baby ➡ bab**ies**

Nouns ending in -f

Add **-s** to nouns ending in -f.

cliff ➡ cliffs

But if you hear a 'v' sound when you say the plural word, spell the plural **-ves**.

loaf ➡ loa**ves**

Nouns ending in -o

Add **-s** to most nouns ending in -o.

photo ➡ photos

But be aware that there are some everyday exceptions.

tomato ➡ tomato**es**

A good dictionary will always tell you how to spell irregular plurals. It's worth making a list of the ones you often need.

● Remember these highly irregular forms:

man ➡ men

woman ➡ women

goose ➡ geese

tooth ➡ teeth

foot ➡ feet

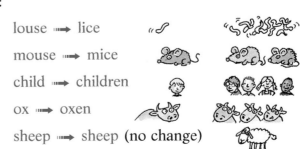

louse ➡ lice

mouse ➡ mice

child ➡ children

ox ➡ oxen

sheep ➡ sheep (no change)

The possessive apostrophe

the keyboard of Fiona = Fiona's keyboard

Rule

- Find the owner   Fiona
- Add the apostrophe   Fiona'
- Add **s** if there isn't one   Fiona's keyboard

Some plural nouns will need **s** to be added but most of them will already have one.

the car of my parents = my parents' car

Rule

- Find the owner   my parents
- Add the apostrophe   my parents'
- Add **s** if there isn't one (There is!)   my parents' car

the boats of the fishermen = the fishermen's boats

Rule

- Find the owner   the fishermen
- Add the apostrophe   the fishermen'
- Add **s** if there isn't one   the fishermen's boats

Activities

9 Write the plurals of these singular nouns. Use a dictionary if you wish.

a) thief _____ f) hero _____
b) city _____ g) bicycle _____
c) woman _____ h) inch _____
d) memory _____ i) potato _____
e) witch _____ j) donkey _____

10 Each sentence below needs one possessive apostrophe. Circle the nouns that require apostrophes and write them correctly punctuated in the spaces on the right.

a) Policemens uniforms are being updated. _____
b) Why are childrens departments so often on the second floors of big stores? _____
c) The small childs handwriting was untidy but the letters were well formed. _____
d) Holidays Unlimited have been inundated with holidaymakers complaints. _____
e) Farmers incomes have been severely affected by the cut in subsidies. _____

11 This exercise tests the spellings set for you to learn on page 9. Circle the correct spelling and write it on the right-hand side.

a) perants   parents   perrants   _____
b) character   charachter   caracter   _____
c) exsercise   exercice   exercise   _____
d) safty   safety   saftey   _____
e) business   buisness   buisnes   _____

12 Antonyms are words that are opposite in meaning. Give the antonyms to these nouns.

a) hope _____ f) wealth _____
b) success _____ g) beginning _____
c) nervousness _____ h) coward _____
d) defeat _____ i) ancestor _____
e) love _____ j) exit _____

13 There are ten collective nouns below. Of what are they collections? Use your dictionary if you wish.

a) a litter of _____ f) a flotilla of _____
b) a ream of _____ g) a horde of _____
c) a plague of _____ h) an anthology of _____
d) a galaxy of _____ i) a host of _____
e) a pride of _____ j) a school of _____

14 Circle the nouns that need apostrophes in the sentences below. (Some sentences may not need any.) Five apostrophes are needed altogether. Write the nouns correctly punctuated in the spaces on the right.

a) It's my parents wedding anniversary on Monday. _____

b) The childrens party was a great success. There were fifteen girls and twelve boys.

_____

c) The boxes of books were stacked at the end of the corridor. _____

d) Mrs Doak groaned, 'Girls voices are so much shriller than boys voices. I have *such* a headache!' _____

e) Year 7s outing has been postponed. _____

15 **Proofreading**

There are twenty errors in the extract below from *Flat Stanley* that have been deliberately introduced for you to identify and correct. Circle the error and write the correction in the spaces on the right.

Breakfast was ready.   _____

'I will go and wake the boy's,' Mrs Lamb-   _____
chop said to her husband, George Lambchop.   _____
Just then their younger sun, arthur, called   _____
from the bedroom he shared with his Brother   _____
Stanley in their new york home.   _____

'Hey! Come and look! Hey!'   _____

Mr and Mrs Lambchop were both very   _____
much in favour of pliteness and careful   _____
speach. 'Hay is for horse's, Arthur, not people,'   _____
Mr Lambchop said as they entered the bed-   _____
room. 'Try to remember that.'   _____

'Excuse me,' Arthur said. 'But look!'   _____

He pointed to Stanleys bed. Across it lay   _____
the enormous bulletin bored that Mr Lamb-   _____
chop had given the boys a christmas ago, so   _____
that they could pin up picturs and massages   _____
and mops. It had fallen, during the might, on   _____
top of stanley.   _____

But Stanley was not hurt. In fact he would   _____
still have been sleeping if he had not been   _____
woken by his brothers shout.   _____

'What's going on here?' he called out   _____
cheerfully from beneath the enormous board.   _____

Mr and Mrs Lambchop hurried to lift it   _____
from the bad.   _____

'Hevens!' said Mrs Lambchop.   _____

'Gosh!' said Arthur. 'Stanley's flat!'   _____

From *Flat Stanley* by Jeff Brown (Puffin 1970)

Verbs

Verbs are **doing** words and **being** words.
They are printed red in this cartoon.

From *The Funday Times*, page 2, in
The Sunday Times, 22 June 1997

Tenses

The action of a verb can take place in the present,
past or future. If Colette's text for her cartoon had
been written in the past tense, it would read like this:

Question: Why were cooks cruel?

Answer: Because they battered fish, beat eggs
and whipped cream.

to batter	Simple present tense		Simple past tense	
	Singular	Plural	Singular	Plural
1st person 2nd person 3rd person	I batter you batter he she } batters it	we batter you batter they batter	I battered you battered he she } battered it	we battered you battered they battered

Usually you add **-ed** to form the simple past tenses but there are some exceptions, for
example:

swam not swimmed
kept not keeped
beat not beated

A dictionary will always warn you if the past tense is irregular.

You can form future tenses and additional present and past tenses with the help of verbs
like to be, to have and to do. You will know at the time which tense is most appropriate
for your purpose. You might like to discuss in pairs the circumstances in which you would
use each of the ones below.

he does jump he is jumping he has jumped	Present tenses
he was jumping he did jump he had jumped	Past tenses
he will jump he will be jumping he will have jumped	Future tenses

Active and passive voice

Active voice

When the subject of the verb is the 'doer', the verb is said to be in the **active voice**:

The man bit the dog.
    subject verb

Passive voice

When the subject or the verb is the 'victim', the verb is said to be in the **passive voice**:

The dog was bitten by the man.
   subject   verb

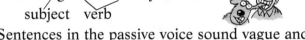

Sentences in the passive voice sound vague and impersonal, which is sometimes useful:

It was decided that everyone present should be searched.

The infinitive (e.g. **to** finish)

The infinitive is the base form of the verb (the starting point) and the one you'll find in a dictionary.

The present participle (e.g. finishing) and the past participle (e.g. finished)

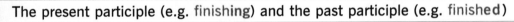

The present participle always ends in **-ing**.
The past participle usually ends in **-ed**, but there are some tricky irregular forms like paid, chosen, seen. If in doubt, check in a dictionary. Irregular past tenses and past participles are always listed.

- The participles can be used to **form tenses**:
  My parents are going to Dublin. (present participle)
  The work will be finished tomorrow. (past participle)

- The participles can also be used **descriptively**:
  The child, sobbing bitterly, was comforted by neighbours.
  (the present participle describes 'the child')
  Unrecognised, he slipped away quietly.
  (the past participle describes 'he')

Always make sure that the participles in your sentences describe the appropriate word:

✗ Giggling helplessly, the parcel was eventually
   delivered by the four girls. (a giggling parcel?)
✔ Giggling helplessly, the four girls eventually
   delivered the parcel.

Activities

16 In pairs, decide whether the **bold** words are nouns or verbs.

a) Our **supply** of file paper is running out. _____

b) I can never **sleep** on trains. _____

c) Try asking for a **refund**. _____

d) **Spot** the difference. _____

e) Now **wash** your hands. _____

17 Compose sentences, using each word first as a noun and then as a verb (two separate sentences for each word).

a) cough _____

b) drive _____

c) delay _____

d) cash _____

e) vote _____

18 Complete the gaps in the table below.

Noun	Verb
enjoyment	enjoy
behaviour	_____
refusal	_____
decision	_____
_____	apologise
_____	revise

19 Complete these past tenses. A dictionary will help.

a) We have _____ all the biscuits. (to eat)

b) Have you _____ your free gift? (to choose)

c) The table was _____ hours ago. (to lay)

d) The window was _____ deliberately. (to break)

e) These rugs are _____ by hand. (to weave)

f) We've _____ all we can afford. (to give)

g) The milk was _____ on the doorstep. (to freeze)

h) They've _____ their coats with them. (to bring)

i) Mary Bryan has _____ the Channel both ways. (to swim)

j) I wish I had _____ that jacket now. (to buy)

20 In small groups discuss why these sentences are unintentionally ridiculous. How should they be rewritten?

a) Roasted slowly, everyone will enjoy these cheap cuts of meat.

_____

b) Sleeping in the garden, a bee stung him.

_____

c) When making cakes, eggs should be at room temperature.

_____

d) Running down the path, a loose paving-stone tripped her up.

_____

e) Turning the corner, their house is on the right.

_____

21 Explain the difference in meaning between these five verbs of saying. Use a dictionary if you wish.

a) to wheedle _____

b) to reiterate _____

c) to retort _____

d) to pontificate _____

e) to exclaim _____

22 Rewrite these sentences in the passive voice.

a) The fox took another hen last night.

_____

b) Nobody knows the whole story.

_____

c) Everyone scored full marks.

_____

d) A spokesman denied the report.

_____

e) The surgeon has postponed the operation.

_____

23 Learn these spellings.

a) annoyed	h) frighten	o) realise/realize
b) approach	i) heard	p) recommend
c) broken	j) interrupt	q) suggest
d) disappoint	k) meant	r) suppose
e) excited	l) mention	s) surprise
f) exhausted	m) murmur	t) tired
g) finish	n) paid	

Pronouns

Identification

Pronouns can replace nouns and so help avoid any unnecessary repetition.

Personal pronouns: I/me, you, he/him, she/her, it, we/us, they/them

Donna saw Megan in town. Donna called out to Megan but Megan didn't hear Donna.

She saw her in town. She called out to her but she didn't hear her.

- You'll see in the example above that pronouns are much vaguer than the nouns they replace. Always check for clarity.
  Donna saw Megan in town. She called out to her but Megan didn't hear her.

- I or me? These can be particularly tricky in combination with a noun or another pronoun. If in doubt, break the combination into its component parts:
  My mother and _____ are going shopping. (I or me?)
  My mother is going shopping. I am going shopping.
  My mother and I are going shopping.

  The present is for you and _____ . (I or me?)
  The present is for you. The present is for me.
  The present is for you and me.

Impersonal pronouns: one, someone, anyone, everyone, no one, somebody, anybody, everybody, nobody, something, anything, everything, nothing

These pronouns are wonderful for generalisations.

- Be careful when you use one. Once you start, you have to keep it up.
  (You is easier to use and less pompous.)
  One can only do one's best but, however hard one tries, one is bound to fail sometimes.

Possessive pronouns: mine, yours, his, hers, ours, theirs

These pronouns show ownership:
  This is mine. That is yours. There is his.

- Don't use apostrophes with possessive pronouns.

Reflexive and emphasising pronouns: myself, yourself, himself, herself, itself, ourselves, yourselves, themselves

The same words can be used in two ways.
Reflexive (refers back to the 'doer' of the verb):
  Sheila has cut herself.
Emphasising (adds emphasis and could be omitted):
  Sheila herself would agree.

● Don't use these as substitutes for personal pronouns:
  ✗ My friends and myself were there.
  ✔ My friends and I were there.
  ✗ They invited my friends and myself.
  ✔ They invited my friends and me.

Relative pronouns: who, whom, that, which

These are linking words:
  There is the man who gave me the parcel.
  There is the girl whom I met last night.
  This is the book that/which I mentioned.

● Who or whom? Break the sentence into two statements:
  There is the man. He gave me the parcel. ⟹ There is the man who gave me the parcel.
  There is the girl. I met her last night. ⟹ There is the girl whom I met last night.

  Who replaces he/she/they.
  Whom replaces him/her/them.

● The relative pronouns whom, that and which can be taken for granted and omitted. However, who must be kept.

Interrogative pronouns: who? whom? what? whose?

These pronouns introduce questions:
  Who asked you? Whom did you meet? Whose is this?

● Who or whom? Anticipate the answer:
  _____ asked you? He/she/they asked me. Use who.
  _____ did you meet? I met him/her/them. Use whom.

Activities

24 I, me, myself?

a) I'm afraid that Shaun and _____ are in disgrace.

b) You and _____ have got to tidy the classroom.

c) I'll do the job _____ .

d) Everybody, including my brother and _____ , had to be interviewed.

e) The headteacher always blames Simone and _____ .

f) I washed _____ from head to foot in icy water.

g) My friend and _____ have collected over £30.

h) Prince Charles shook hands gravely with Charlotte and _____ .

i) My parents and _____ used to live in Hampshire.

j) I'm going to give _____ a break when I've finished this.

25 Supply the appropriate possessive pronouns. (Remember no possessive apostrophes are needed.)

a) I used **your pen** by mistake.

By mistake, I used _____ .

b) I prefer **my essay**.

I prefer _____ .

c) **Jake's entry** was the best in the region.

_____ was the best in the region.

d) I'm glad you had a good holiday. **Our holiday** was a disaster.

I'm glad you had a good holiday. _____ was a disaster.

e) Have you finished **your project** yet?

Have you finished _____ yet?

26 There is at least one error in each of these sentences. Circle all the errors and write the corrections in the spaces on the right.

a) You and I knows him well. _____

b) The pen was her's and not Ian's. _____

c) Naturally John and myself volunteered. _____

d) No one says what they really think on these occasions. _____

e) What one suffers in childhood continues to affect you for the rest of your life.

_____

27 Who or whom?

a) _____ is coming to your party?

b) _____ knows the password?

c) _____ can we trust to keep it secret?

d) _____ did you see?

e) _____ told you this?

28 Combine each pair of statements into a single, well constructed sentence. Use **who**, **whom**, **which** or **that** as linking words.

a) She was a lady. Very few people ever got to know her well.

_____

b) That's the motor-bike. I shall buy it if I win the jackpot.

_____

c) I want you to meet a neighbour. She has been very kind to me.

_____

d) I have a friend. He is a brilliant chess-player.

_____

e) Cherrill is a person. I admire her very much.

_____

29 **Proofreading**

There are twenty deliberate errors in the paragraph below for you to find and identify. Circle each error and write corrections in the spaces on the right.

Fammillys can be over-protective were elderly relations is conserned. Most elderly poeple are perfickly capable of looking aftr theirselves and they shoud be aloud to do so. We must rember that they value their independence as much as we value our's, and we need to remind ourselfs regularly that they have the right to be in charge of their own lifes. They will be justifiably anoyed if we interfere at every oppertunity. That is not to surjest that health and saftey are not important but to emphasise that tact and diplomacy are important too. There is a lesson here for you and I and every one else whom reads this.

_____

_____

_____

_____

_____

_____

_____

_____

_____

_____

_____

_____

Adjectives

Identification

> **Adjectives** are **describing words**. They tell us more about nouns and pronouns.

The pony plunged forward but the strong, heavy hand held the pretty creature back with force almost enough to break its jaw whilst the whip still cut into him. It was a dreadful sight to me, for I knew what fearful pain it gave that delicate little mouth.

From *Black Beauty* by Anna Sewell (Armada Classics)

All these words printed in purple are adjectives.

It was dreadful.

She came fourth.

Pass me those mugs.

I've lost my coursework.

Each pupil won a medal.

Whose shoebag is it?

What rubbish!

He's the man whose car was stolen.

Deirdre loves Italian ice-cream.

Nouns can be used as adjectives to describe other nouns:

There'll be a play rehearsal after school.

Will you pass the fitness test?

Groups of words can be hyphenated and used as adjectives:

I'm tired of his couldn't-care-less attitude.

Participles

Present and past participles can be used to describe nouns and pronouns:

The child, sobbing bitterly, was comforted by neighbours.
Unrecognised, he slipped away quietly.

Remember that participles are very active describing words – adjectives with muscle, you might say. They are still verbs even when they're doing the work of adjectives.

a walking stick
simple adjective

a walking stick
present participle

Comparison of adjectives

You'll already be familiar with the comparative and superlative forms of adjectives in everyday speech, even if the grammatical terminology is unfamiliar:

Comparative: He is richer than I am.
Superlative: She is the richest girl I know.

Add **-er** and **-est** to short adjectives:

rich ➡ rich**er** ➡ rich**est**

Use **more** and **most** with long adjectives:

beautiful ➡ **more** beautiful ➡ **most** beautiful

- Be careful not to mix the two methods of forming the comparative and superlative:
  rich**er** (not **more** richer)
  most beautiful (not **most** beautiful**lest**)

- Remember the three irregular adjectives:
  good ➡ better ➡ best
  bad ➡ worse ➡ worst
  many ➡ more ➡ most

- Remember that some words are absolute and don't have a comparative and superlative form. For example, something is either unique or it's not.

Activities

30 Learn these spellings.

a) beautiful

b) careful

c) certain

d) desperate

e) different

f) difficult

g) embarrassing

h) excellent

i) favourite

j) grateful

k) honest

l) humorous

m) interesting

n) lonely

o) necessary

p) pleasant

q) possible

r) ridiculous

s) separate

t) useful

31 Ten of these sentences need adjustment because the comparative and superlative have been wrongly formed. Circle the errors and write the correct forms in the spaces alongside. Tick the sentences which are correct.

a) She is the most beautiful woman I have ever seen. _____

b) Do you think Guy is more handsomer than Miles? _____

c) Of the two boys, Edward is the more courteous. _____

d) This dog is the most worst behaved dog we've ever had. _____

e) The most usefullest gadget I possess is my potato peeler. _____

f) He promised to do gooder work in future. _____

g) You are my very bestest friend. _____

h) Sally is the least helpful member of the class. _____

i) I think lilac has the most loveliest scent of all. _____

j) You are the kindest girl I know. _____

k) The house has been described as the most unique in America. _____

l) Their house is the most grandest I've ever seen. _____

m) You'll find roast pork is more tastier if you add a sprig of rosemary. _____

n) Gavin is the impatientest person I know. _____

32 Supply the remaining letters in these adjectives derived from names of countries, islands and cities.

a) __ __ __ c __ bulbs (Holland)

b) __ __ __ __ __ __ n chocolate (Belgium)

c) __ __ __ __ sh bacon (Denmark)

d) __ __ n __ cat (Isle of Man)

e) __ __ __ __ t __ __ __ blinds (Venice)

f) __ a __ __ __ __ __ __ fashions (Paris)

g) __ __ __ __ w __ __ __ __ __ accent (Glasgow)

h) __ __ __ __ __ __ u __ __ __ __ __ humour (Liverpool)

i) __ __ __ __ e __ __ __ __ sailors (Norway)

j) __ __ __ __ __ __ __ h dancing (Spain)

33 With the help of your dictionary, match the appropriate adjectives in the box with the definitions below.

asinine	canine	lupine	vulpine
aquiline	feline	porcine	
bovine	leonine	equine	

a) like a cat _____

b) like a dog _____

c) like a horse _____

d) like a lion _____

e) like a fox _____

f) like a cow _____

g) like an eagle _____

h) like an ass _____

i) like a wolf _____

j) like a pig _____

34 Give the antonyms (opposites) of these adjectives.

a) rude _____

b) lazy _____

c) vague _____

d) modest _____

e) innocent _____

f) fertile _____

g) voluntary _____

h) rural _____

i) confident _____

j) heavy _____

35 Complete the gaps in the table below. Use a dictionary if you wish.

Noun	Verb	Adjective
_____	_____	decisive
_____	obey	_____
success	_____	_____
_____	pity	_____
_____	_____	sympathetic

36 Circle the correct spellings and write them in the spaces provided.

a) embarassing embarrassing embarressing _____

b) neccessary necesary necessary _____

c) difficult differcult difficalt _____

d) exellent excellant excellent _____

e) plesant pleasent pleasant _____

f) usfull useful usefull _____

g) onest honist honest _____

h) careful carfull carefull _____

i) possible possable posable _____

j) greatful gratefull grateful _____

Adverbs

Identification

> **Adverbs** usually describe verbs.

The telephone was answered immediately. (adverb of **time**)
Patrick promised to wait for me here. (adverb of **place**)
Boma gulped the milk greedily. (adverb of **manner**)

See how adverbs can add atmosphere to this description:

> I knocked and waited. Ten seconds passed. The door swung open in front of me and there stood Captain Hughes. 'Enter,' he said.

> I knocked timidly and waited. Ten seconds passed – too quickly. Then the door swung open menacingly in front of me and there stood Captain Hughes. 'Enter,' he said softly.

● Sometimes adverbs can describe other adverbs:
   Ten seconds passed **too** quickly.
   The telephone was answered **almost** immediately.
   Boma gulped the milk **really** greedily.

   Too, almost and really are adverbs of **degree**.

● Adverbs of degree can also describe adjectives:
   The poor cat was almost dead.
   Are you quite sure?
   I am very sorry.
   The road is extremely dangerous.

The adverb game

Reinforce your understanding of adverbs of manner by playing the adverb game.

1 A volunteer leaves the classroom while the rest of the class (quickly and quietly) choose a good adverb to mime. (Adverbs like nervously, shyly, angrily, cheerfully and energetically work well.)

2 The volunteer is called in and has to guess the adverb after asking people to mime actions in the manner of the chosen adverb. (Comb your hair like this. Read a book like this. Walk to the blackboard like this. ...)

3 The last person to mime before the volunteer correctly guesses the adverb takes over, and the game begins all over again.

Comparison of adverbs

Forming the comparative and superlative of adverbs is quite straightforward.

Add **-er** and **-est** to most short adverbs:

Matthew works hard➡harder➡hardest.

Use **more** and **most** with longer adverbs:

Anna dances gracefully➡**more** gracefully➡**most** gracefully.

● Be careful not to mix the two methods of forming the comparative and superlative:

harder (not **more** harder)

most gracefully (not **most** gracefull**estly**).

● Remember the four irregular adverbs:

badly➡worse➡worst

little ➡ less ➡ least

much➡more➡most

well➡better➡best

Activities

37 Learn these spellings.

a) absolutely

b) accidentally

c) apparently

d) conscientiously

e) definitely

f) enthusiastically

g) eventually

h) extremely

i) gradually

j) immediately

k) immensely

l) occasionally

m) originally

n) probably

o) really

p) recently

q) scarcely

r) severely

s) sincerely

t) usually

38 Circle any errors in the use of adverbs you can find in the sentences below. Write the corrections in the spaces provided.

a) When Jim saw the police coming, he ran real quick. _____

_____

b) The more sooner we arrive, the more sooner we can leave. _____

_____

c) The candidate who performed the most badly was Louise. _____

_____

d) I'm sure he's done it wrong. _____

_____

e) The calmier you take life, the longer you'll live. _____

_____

39 Find the three adverbs that are used in the passage below and write them in the boxes. Explain briefly what each adverb adds to the meaning of the passage.

Dermot glanced casually down the corridor before slipping the stolen key into the lock of Room 396. He then set about a systematic and thorough search of all possible hiding-places. He knew exactly what he was looking for and he intended to find it.

40 Change the nouns below into adjectives and adverbs. Write a sentence next to each noun, adjective and adverb to show each word in use.

a) noun	hope	
adjective		
adverb		
b) noun	effort	
adjective		
adverb		
c) noun	danger	
adjective		
adverb		

41 **Vocabulary exercise**

Tick the definitions you think come closest to the meaning of the adverbs on the left.

a) surreptitiously: delicately ☐ furtively ☐ jokingly ☐

b) voluntarily: by choice ☐ by force ☐ by popular vote ☐

c) seldom: quite often ☐ hardly ever ☐ not at all ☐

42 Circle the correct spellings and write them in the spaces provided.

a) usully usally usually _____

b) absoloutly absolutly absolutely _____

c) scarsly scarcely scarsley _____

d) really realy rearly _____

e) severly severely severley _____

f) extremeley extreamly extremely _____

g) sincerly sincerley sincerely _____

h) accidently acidentally accidentally _____

i) originally origionally oroginally _____

j) immensely immensly immensley _____

Conjunctions

Identification

> **Conjunctions** are **joining** words.

Co-ordinating conjunctions join parallel words and word groups in an equal, balanced way.

fish and chips
an untidy house but a happy home
take it or leave it

Subordinating conjunctions join sentences by making some less important than others.

Elaine deserves to do well.
She works hard.
Elaine deserves to do well because she works hard.

      |
  main statement

My mother hates spiders.
She's promised to look after my tarantula.
I shall be in Portsmouth.
Although my mother hates spiders, **she's promised to look after my tarantula** while
I'm in Portsmouth.

            main statement

Here are some useful subordinating conjunctions to use in your own writing when you want to combine short, jerky sentences into more effective longer ones:

after	even if	unless
although	for	until
as	if	when
as if	in case	where
as long as	since	whether
as though	so that	whenever
because	that	wherever
before	thought	while

Prepositions

Identification

What are prepositions? They are little words that show how one thing relates to another. Here are some that indicate position, time, direction, possession and manner:

about	beneath	into	towards
above	beside	like	under
across	between	near	until
after	by	of	up
against	down	on	upon
among	for	over	with
at	from	past	within
before	in	round	without
below	inside	to	

You will find that when a word is being used as a preposition (some of the words in the list above can also be used as adverbs and subordinating conjunctions) it will usually be followed by a noun or a pronoun:

> This novel was written by Michael Carson.
> Give that to me.

Using prepositions correctly requires care.

- If ever you are uncertain which preposition to use with certain constructions, your dictionary will help you:

  > merge _____ ? ➡ merge into
  > resort _____ ? ➡ resort to
  > hint _____ ? ➡ hint at

- Remember that prepositions can have a powerful effect on meaning:

  > to agree to = to give your consent
  > to agree with = to share someone's opinion

- In **conversation** you would probably say:

  > He's a man I have enormous respect for.

  In **formal speech** and in **writing**, you would say or write:

  > He is a man for whom I have enormous respect.

- Don't skimp on prepositions on formal occasions.

  In **conversation** you would probably say:

  > Sean is a passionate supporter and campaigner for Animal Rights.

  In **formal speech** and in **writing**, you would say or write:

  > Sean is a passionate supporter of and campaigner for Animal Rights.

Activities

43 Combine each group of sentences into a single sentence using **and**, **but**, **or** as appropriate.

a) I am sorry. I can't marry you. That's my final answer.

_____

b) Will you drive? Will you go by train?

_____

c) Janine gave in. She dialled the number.

_____

d) We could go to Paris. We could go to Marseilles. We can't afford to go to both.

_____

e) William longs to leave London. He doesn't think it will ever be possible.

_____

44 Use an appropriate subordinating conjunction to join these sentences. (If you like a challenge, try to avoid using any conjunction more than once.)

a) You want to lose weight. Eat less.

_____

b) I should like to help you. I am too busy.

_____

c) Stephen goes. The dog follows.

_____

d) You are so kind. I want to give you this.

_____

e) You went out of the door. Michael phoned.

_____

45 Write a story (at least 100 words long) which involves a cat, a torch and a policeman. Use no more than eight sentences.

_____

_____

_____

_____

_____

_____

_____

_____

_____

_____

_____

16 Supply the appropriate preposition. (Use your dictionary if you wish.)

a) to sympathise _____   f) to triumph _____

b) to object _____   g) to concentrate _____

c) to consist _____   h) to collaborate _____

d) to revolve _____   i) to gossip _____

e) to have an aptitude _____   j) to benefit _____

17 Compose a sentence for each of the expressions below.

a) look at _____

b) look into _____

c) look after _____

d) look up _____

e) laugh at _____

f) laugh off _____

g) talk to _____

h) talk about _____

i) talk round _____

j) talk over _____

18 Rewrite these colloquial sentences to avoid having the preposition at the end.

a) This is the moment Charlotte has been longing for.

_____

b) Croquet is not a game Sam has taken much interest in.

_____

c) Who did you write to?

_____

d) Smoking is a habit Paula has always disapproved of.

_____

e) It's his father he's afraid of.

_____

19 A preposition has been left out of each of these sentences. Indicate with an insertion mark (∧) where the missing preposition should be inserted and write the preposition in the space provided.

a) Nobody knew of his allergy and intolerance of penicillin.   _____

b) Emily is both fascinated and curious about insects.   _____

c) Kieran has learned to cope and not to be ashamed of his disability.   _____

d) The governors objected and complained about the plan.   _____

e) All the parents were disgusted and angry at the result of the appeal.   _____

Sentences, phrases and clauses

What are sentences? What are clauses? What are phrases? Let us begin with some working definitions.

> **Sentences** are grammatically self-contained and make complete sense on their own. They have at least one verb with a subject (see page 15).

Sentences can be statements, questions, commands or exclamations.
All sentences begin with a capital letter and end with either a full stop, a question mark or an exclamation mark.

Statement: **I**'ll climb down in a minute.
Question: **W**hat are you doing up there?
Command: **B**e careful!
Exclamation: **W**hat a dreadful child you are!

● The verb in a command has a subject which is 'understood'. That is, it's not actually said but everyone knows what it is:

(you) Be careful!

> **Phrases** are groups of words **without** finite verbs which don't make sense outside the context of the sentence.

at the weekend
on the bus
singing in the bath

● The present participle (for example, singing), the past participle (for example, sung), and the infinitive (for example, to sing) are non-finite parts of the verb when used on their own and not as part of tenses with subjects (see pages 14 and 15).

> Subordinate **clauses** are groups of words **with** finite verbs, but which don't make complete sense without the rest of the sentence.

after I've done my homework
which has a sad ending
that she will come

Adjectives, adjectival phrases, adjectival clauses

> Adjectives describe nouns and pronouns, and so do adjectival phrases and adjectival clauses.

Phrases and clauses can do the work of adjectives, adverbs and nouns:

a bad-tempered teacher (adjective)
a teacher with a bad temper (adjectival phrase)
a teacher who has a bad temper (adjectival clause)

Some more **adjectival phrases**:
Is he the comedian with the silly voice?
Sally was wearing a dress of dark-red velvet.
Megan looked round the door, smiling mischievously.

- Always make sure the adjectival phrase is describing the **right** noun or pronoun:
  ✗ 1990 Mini wanted by a learner-driver in good condition.

  ✔ 1990 Mini in good condition wanted by learner-driver.

Some more **adjectival clauses**:
Do you know anyone who can mend canvas canoes?
The builder whom you recommended has moved to Ipswich.
Is this the video that you wanted to borrow?
Is this the video which you wanted to borrow?
Gandhi was a leader whose courage was widely admired.
Can you remember that Christmas when we all had flu?
This is the house where Shakespeare was born.

- Whom, what and which can always be omitted and simply be 'understood' to be there.

- Can you see how a pair of commas around an adjectival clause affects the meaning?
  A The workmen, who wore safety helmets, were unhurt.
  B The workmen who wore safety helmets were unhurt.
  Question: In which sentence are all the workmen unhurt?
  (Answer at foot of page.)

Answer: All the workmen in the first sentence escaped injury. They were sensible. All wore safety helmets.

Activities

50 The exercise below contains ten complete sentences (deliberately written without initial capitals and full stops in order to disguise them!). Can you identify them? Tick each complete sentence.

a) feeling very tearful and miserable

b) both children are doing very well at school

c) giggling and whispering in the corner

d) he has been promoted

e) we know her well

f) their house has been sold

g) because they want to go on holiday

h) the story seemed rather far-fetched

i) they are not here

j) they apologised

k) it cost me £2

l) as they rushed down the slope

m) with every intention of making me trip up

n) the headmaster will be late this morning

o) your car looks very clean

51 Punctuate the sentences that follow with a full stop, a question mark or exclamation mark as necessary.

a) Would you like me to open a window ____

b) Leave my bag alone ____

c) He's a very kind man ____

d) I should like to ask you some questions ____

e) Oh, no, I've lost my car keys ____

f) What's the time ____

g) Do you know Michael well ____

h) Fiona is playing netball today ____

i) Have you decided what to do ____

j) It's a pity that you didn't tell me this before ____

52 Incorporate these phrases and clauses into sentences.

a) sneezing and coughing

_____

b) if I can

_____

c) I think he is learning to play the flute

_____

d) with a nasty smile

_____

e) at Christmas

_____

53 Compose sentences to incorporate the adjectival phrases and clauses that follow. Underline the nouns and pronouns described.

a) licking a lollipop

_____

b) of marigolds

_____

c) where Alan used to work

_____

d) who never says anything nasty about anyone

_____

e) whose mother is very strict

_____

_____

54 Join these pairs of sentences by making one sentence in each pair into an adjectival clause.

a) My mother knows nothing about antiques. She has run a successful chain of antique shops for years.

_____

_____

b) I've just finished reading a collection of short stories. Bill Greenwell recommended the book.

_____

_____

c) The Prime Minister drove past the terraced house. He was born there.

_____

_____

55 Show by insertion marks (∧) where commas should be added in these sentences. Here are some examples of how commas are used with adjectival phrases beginning with participles.

Smiling warmly, Kendall come to meet us.

She led the way, talking excitedly, into the kitchen.

We saw the vase, broken into tiny fragments.

a) Waving excitedly the little boy looked out of the window.

b) They arrived home at midnight covered in mud.

c) Knitting furiously the woman glared at everyone who came into the compartment.

d) Alan drove through the gates carefully and then coming to a gentle halt beside the pond heaved a sigh of relief.

e) Humiliated by the enemy the soldiers regrouped.

Adverbs, adverbial phrases, adverbial clauses

Time

The door was opened **when?**

           verb

The door was opened immediately. (adverb of time)

The door was opened in a flash. (adverbial phrase of time)

The door was opened while I was still ringing the bell. (adverbial clause of time)

Place

The group should meet **where?**

           verb

Meet me here. (adverb of place)

Meet me at this spot. (adverbial phrase of place)

Meet me where we are now. (adverbial clause of place)

Manner

My father nodded **how?**

           verb

My father nodded approvingly. (adverb of manner)

My father nodded with approval. (adverbial phrase of manner)

My father nodded as if he approved. (adverbial clause of manner)

● Notice that a comma is usually needed if the adverb, adverbial phrase or adverbial clause comes before the verb it describes:

    Immediately, the door was opened.

    In a flash, the door was opened.

    While I was still ringing the bell, the door was opened.

Types of adverbial clause

We have just seen three of the questions that adverbial clauses can answer. There are nine questions altogether. Here is a complete list:

Question	Example		Type of adverbial clause
when?	Wait until the clock strikes eight.		Time
where?	We can go wherever we like.		Place
how?	You all look as though you've seen a ghost.		Manner
why?	We left because it started to rain.		Reason
on what condition?	I'll give you £10 if you get a good school report.		Condition
even though...?	Simon is still in debt although he's started to economise.		Concession
to what purpose?	The twins saved really hard so that they could buy a camera.		Purpose
with what result?	Tracey played truant so often that she has been expelled.		Result
to what extent?	Harold is much more loyal than James (is).		Degree

- Adverbial clauses of degree describe adjectives. In the example above, we are discussing to what extent Harold is **loyal**. All the rest describe verbs.

- Can you see the difference in function here?
    This is the house where I was born. (adjectival clause)
    Stay where I tell you. (adverbial clause of place)

Activities

56 Match each clause from the first column with an adverbial clause from the second. (Use each clause once only.) Write out each complete sentence, correctly punctuated.

Charlotte disliked the novel

aren't you allowed to go out

my kitten follows me

the roads became impassable

rest for a little while

until the exams are over

although rain had not been forecast

as you've had a nasty shock

because it was too violent

wherever I go

_____

_____

_____

_____

_____

57 Combine these pairs by making one sentence in each pair into an adverbial clause. Adapt the wording as required.

a) The alarm bell went off. Simon got up reluctantly.

_____

b) I go to the dentist regularly. I am terrified of toothache.

_____

c) Have you no one to go with you? Come with me.

_____

d) Elise is doing very little work. She's bound to fail.

_____

e) You may not like her very much. You should visit her.

_____

58 Rewrite the sentences below, substituting adverbs or adverbial phrases for the **bold** adverbial clauses.

a) **If we're lucky**, we'll get tickets.

_____

b) **When the form is completed**, post it to DVLA, Swansea.

_____

c) **Although she was willing**, the authorities would not let her help.

_____

d) The old lady died **because she had eaten nothing for weeks**.

_____

e) The receptionist looked at me **as though she sympathised**.

_____

59 These sentences are clumsily constructed. Rewrite them so that the intended meaning is absolutely clear.

a) Your hair needs cutting badly.

_____

b) Nobody was injured as we hoped.

_____

c) Erected to the memory of John Ferris who was drowned at sea by his loving family.

_____

_____

60 **Like** is a preposition and will be followed by a noun or pronoun.

As is a subordinating conjunction, introducing an adverbial clause of manner, time, reason or degree.

Only two of the sentences below use **like** correctly. Find these two and tick them.

a) It happened exactly like I've described.

b) Jennifer looks like an angel in this photograph.

c) Like I say, I was miles away at the time.

d) I can't talk to people like you do.

e) Like most shy people, Trevor blushes easily.

61 Use insertion marks to show where commas should be inserted in these sentences. (Not all the sentences require commas.)

For example: Although he's really ill he won't rest.

               Although he's really ill $\wedge$ he won't rest.

a) If you like you can stay with us.

b) When James started school he hated it.

c) I like him because he makes me laugh.

d) Unless you get a move on you'll miss the bus.

e) We'll have supper when we've finished.

f) After you've washed up will you help me with this letter?

g) Since you're here you may as well sit down.

h) He was late because he'd overslept.

i) I'll come although I'm not very keen.

j) He should if all goes well be promoted this year.

Nouns, noun phrases, noun clauses

> Nouns do five different jobs in sentences. Noun phrases and noun clauses can do all these jobs too.

1 | They can be the **subject of the verb**.

To find the subject of the verb, put **who?** or **what?** in front of it:

James hit me.
Question: **Who** hit me? Answer: James
The noun James is the **subject** of the verb hit.

Anxiety is making her ill.
Question: **What** is making her ill? Answer: Anxiety
The noun anxiety is the **subject** of the verb is making.

Noun phrases and noun clauses can be the subjects of verbs too:

Being so anxious is making her ill. (noun phrase)
That she is so anxious is making her ill. (noun clause)

● Remember always to match subjects and verbs. Singular subjects need singular verbs; plural subjects need plural verbs:

Being so anxious and being so overworked are making her ill.

2 | They can be the **object of the verb**.

To find the object of the verb, put **whom?** or **what?** after the verb:

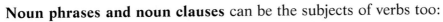

I hit James.
Question: I hit **whom**? Answer: James
The noun James is the **object** of the verb hit.

Noun phrases and noun clauses can be the objects of verbs too:

I strongly resented having to apologise. (noun phrase)
I could accept that I had to apologise. (noun clause)

3 They can be **the complement of six verbs.**

To be, to seem, to appear, to become, to remain, to stay take complements to complete them and not objects.

All the family are acrobats.

● To feel (when meaning to seem) and to turn and to grow (when meaning to become) also take complements:

He has turned traitor.

Noun phrases and noun clauses can be complements too:

Her advice is to eat plenty of cabbage. (noun phrase)
Her advice is that you should eat plenty of cabbage. (noun clause)

4 They can be **in apposition** to a noun or pronoun.

Look at this sentence:

My boyfriend, **Shaun**, loves beefburgers.

The words my boyfriend and Shaun refer to the same person. You could leave out one of the references altogether:

My boyfriend loves beefburgers.
Shaun loves beefburgers.

The second reference in our example is said to be **in apposition** to the first one. Shaun is in apposition to my boyfriend.

My cat, **Benson**, is getting lazy.

Double-check there are two ways of referring to the same animal:

✔ My cat is getting lazy.
✔ Benson is getting lazy.

Noun phrases and noun clauses can be in apposition too:

Her hobby, **collecting buttons**, takes all her time. (noun phrase)
Everybody believed the rumour **that you had emigrated.** (noun clause)
It was rumoured **that you had emigrated.** (noun clause)

5 They can **follow a preposition.**

We object to homework. (noun)
Olga dreams of returning to Russia. (noun phrase)
We are amazed at what you have achieved. (noun clause)

Activities

62 Replace all the **bold** noun clauses with noun phrases.

a) The doctor is not sure about **what has caused the rash**.

_____

b) I'll never forget **how kind she has been to us**.

_____

c) **That the school will have to close** now seems certain.

_____

d They've found out **what we have planned to do**.

_____

e) This is **what I recommend**.

_____

63 In **bold** in the sentences below are:

- an adjectival clause
- an adverbial clause of place
- a noun clause subject of a verb
- a noun clause object of a verb
- a noun clause complement of a verb

Try to identify each one correctly.

a) **Where he lives** is a mystery. _____

b) The house **where he lives** is enormous. _____

c) That is **where he lives**. _____

d) I don't know **where he lives**. _____

e) It is very isolated **where he lives**. _____

64 Punctuate these sentences correctly by placing a pair of commas around each phrase apposition.

a) Michael Carson the novelist lives in Ireland.

_____

b) My boyfriend the brother of my sister's boyfriend is backpacking around Australia for five months.

_____

_____

c) Our form teacher Mrs Green is popular with everyone.

_____

_____

d) Their new song 'I'll never forget you' is zooming up the charts.

_____

_____

e) My packed lunch of an apple and a marmite sandwich wouldn't keep a grasshopper alive.

_____

_____

65 **General revision exercise**

Julius Caesar has just been assassinated by Brutus and the rest of the conspirators. Unwisely, they have allowed Antony, one of his supporters, to speak at his funeral. Antony has agreed not to blame the conspirators (openly!).

Antony: Good friends, sweet friends, let me not stir you up   1
        To such a sudden flood of mutiny.
        They that have done this deed are honourable.
        What private griefs they have, alas, I know not,
        That made them do it. They are wise and honourable,   5
        And will, no doubt, with reasons answer you.
        I come not, friends, to steal away your hearts.
        I am no orator, as Brutus is,
        But, as you know me all, a plain blunt man,
        That love my friend; and that they know full well   10
        That gave me public leave to speak of him.

From *Illustrated Shakespeare: Julius Caesar* (ed. Neil King), Act 3, Scene ii, by William Shakespeare (Stanley Thornes 1990)

a) What part of speech is 'honourable' in line 3? _____

b) Is the first sentence of Antony's speech (lines 1 and 2) a statement, a command or a question? _____

c) 'They **that have done this deed** are honourable' (line 3) Is the clause in **bold** a noun, adjectival or adverbial one?

_____

d) '**What private griefs they have**, alas, I know not, **that made them do it**.' (lines 4 and 5) What is the function of the clauses in **bold**?

_____

_____

e) Is 'leave' (line 11) a noun or a verb here? _____

f) There is no secret about who killed Caesar and the crowd knows their names. What is the effect, however, of Antony referring to them repeatedly as 'they' and 'them'?

_____

_____

_____

g) Antony is not really a 'plain blunt man' (line 9) as he pretends to be here. In what ways has he deliberately made his speech sound like the speech of a plain, blunt man?

_____

_____

_____

Synthesis

In this section we shall be practising different ways of varying the construction of sentences and of combining short jerky sentences into longer and more fluent ones. Here are seven useful ways.

1 Try using **co-ordinating conjunctions**: and, but, or

> I should like to come to your party. I can't come.
> I should like to come to your party **but** I can't.

2 Try using a pair of **correlative conjunctions**: either...or, neither...nor, both...and, not only...but also

> You are a coward. You are a liar.
> You are **not only** a coward **but also** a liar.

3 Try using **subordinating conjunctions**: as, when, before, since, because, although, if, and so on.

> Simon's attention wandered. He was usually conscientious.
> Simon's attention wandered **although** he was usually conscientious.

4 Try using **relative pronouns** and **relative adjectives**: who, whom, that, which, whose, when, where, why

> Jane is an actress. She is nervous on stage.
> Jane is an actress **who** is nervous on stage.

5 Try reducing one sentence to a single word or phrase

> My mother panicked. She called for help.
> **In a panic**, my mother called for help.

6 Try using **a participle**: -ing, -ed

> Martina peered in the mirror. She brushed on mascara.
> **Peering in the mirror**, Martina brushed on mascara.

7 Try using **a semi-colon**: ;

- Join only **sentences** with a semi-colon – not phrases, clauses or one sentence and just a part of another one.

- Both sentences must have a close connection in sense:
> Nick is exhausted. He has been cleaning his bedroom.
> Nick is exhausted; he has been cleaning his bedroom.

The structure of sentences

There are basically three sentence patterns.

The simple sentence: one main clause (no subordinate clauses)

The simple sentence contains just one finite verb and is therefore just one clause, making a central statement:

We enjoyed the trip to Stratford.

The complex sentence: one main clause and at least one subordinate clause

If you add at least one noun, adjectival or adverbial clause to a simple sentence, then you have a complex sentence:

We enjoyed the trip to Stratford (although the weather was dreadful).

The compound sentence: at least two main clauses (subordinate clauses optional)

If you join two or more simple sentences together with **and**, **but**, **or**, you will have a compound sentence:

We enjoyed the trip to Stratford and we'd like to go again.

Compound sentences can have, in addition, any number of subordinate clauses:

We enjoyed the trip to Stratford (although the weather was dreadful) and we'd like to go again (if there is time) (before exams begin).

Activities

66 Join by using **and**, **but**, **or**.

a) We could watch a video at home tonight. We could go to the cinema.

_____

b) We have complete trust in our family doctor. We don't want to go to anyone else.

_____

c) You can vote labour. I shall vote Liberal Democrat.

_____

d) Mr Perrins is strict. He is fair.

_____

e) You can take history. You can take geography. You can't take both.

_____

67 Use any subordinating conjunctions from the box to join these sentences. (You may rearrange the order of the information given.)

after	because	since	when
although	before	so that	where
as	even if	that	whether
as if	for	though	whenever
as long as	if	unless	wherever
as though	in case	until	while

a) He is going to be sacked. He has a wife and ten children. He sees the boss later this morning. He's hopeless at his job.

_____

_____

b) I shall be in Germany. I should love to see your new house. I shall have to decline the invitation.

_____

_____

c) We had read 120 books each. We agreed. John Beresford should get the fiction prize. It was a hard decision.

_____

_____

d) Sarah said. They have relations there. They can sell their house. Her family will be moving to Cheshire.

_____

_____

e) I am mistaken. You owe me £10.

_____

58 Write up these notes on Roald Dahl as a smooth paragraph of seven sentences. You may change the wording and the order of the material but take care not to omit any of the information given.

Roald Dahl – one of the most successful and popular children's writers – read by children all around the world – books include 'James and the Giant Peach', 'Charlie and the Chocolate Factory', 'Fantastic Mr Fox', 'The BFG' and 'The Witches' (won the Whitbread Award in 1983) – died November 1990, aged 74 – parents from Norway – Roald Dahl born in Wales in 1916 – educated at Repton School – savage beatings – headmaster was Geoffrey Fisher, future Archbishop of Canterbury (crowned Queen Elizabeth) – at 18 joined the Shell Oil Company – after three years' training in England posted in 1936 to East Africa – on outbreak of World War Two joined RAF as fighter pilot – badly injured over Libyan Desert – six months in hospital – but returned to flying – invalided out in 1941 – in 1942 appointed Assistant Air Attaché in Washington – began writing short stories in Washington

Direct and indirect speech

Direct speech quotes the actual words of the speaker:

"I'm sorry I kicked your car," the young lad said to Mrs Evans.

Indirect speech reports what was said (some people call it 'reported speech' for this reason):

✔ The young lad apologised to Mrs Evans for kicking her car.

✔ The young lad told Mrs Evans that he was sorry that he had kicked her car.

In this section, we practise writing in both forms so that you can use either form with confidence when appropriate in your own writing.

Direct speech

See how Michelle Magorian uses direct speech in this early extract from *Goodnight Mister Tom*:

> "Cor!" gasped Willie. "Ain't it fine!"
>
> "Best to be comfortable," said Tom, and he gave a short cough to hide his pleasure.
>
> "Proper job," agreed George.

From *Goodnight Mister Tom* by Michelle Magorian (Puffin 1983)

You can see the advantages of direct speech. Reading this, it's as if you were there, eavesdropping on the conversation in the newly dug air-raid shelter. You can 'hear' the voices of the speakers as well as their words.

Punctuating direct speech needs some care. There are four basic patterns (which you can use as models).

1 | Speech first, narrative second |

"I am sorry," he said. (statement)

"Why did you do it?" she asked. (question)

"Come here!" ordered Mr Evans. (command)

● Inverted commas enclose the words actually spoken and the punctuation that goes with it (a comma, a question mark or an exclamation mark).

● Note how the rest of the sentence (the narrative) continues with an initial small letter because the sentence **as a whole** is not yet finished.

2 Narrative first, speech second

He said, "I'm sorry."

She asked, "Why did you do it?"

Mr Evans ordered, "Come here!"

- As before, inverted commas enclose the actual words spoken.
- A comma marks the transition from narrative to speech.
- Each sentence of speech begins with a capital letter.
- The full stop goes inside the inverted commas.
- No other full stop is needed.

3 A sentence of speech interrupted by narrative

"I'm sorry," he said, "that I kicked your car."

"Why," she asked, "did you do it?"

"Come here," ordered Mr Evans, "and let me have a look at you!"

- A comma marks the transition from speech to narrative.
- A comma marks the transition from narrative back to speech.
- An initial small letter is used when speech is resumed because it's **not** a new sentence being started.

4 Two or more sentences in one speech

"I'm sorry that I kicked your car," he said. "I don't know what made me do it. I've never kicked a car before."

- Inverted commas indicate where the words quoted begin and end. They do **not** have to enclose every single sentence spoken within that speech!

The layout of direct speech

Look at how dialogue is presented in the novels that you read. Look again at the extract from *Goodnight Mister Tom* opposite.

- A new line is taken every time there is a change of speaker (even if only one word is spoken).
- The beginning of each speech is indented slightly.

Activities

69 Punctuate these sentences. (All are 'speech first, narrative second'.)

a) are you feeling better now she asked kindly

_____

b) we shall be moving in the summer announced ruth

_____

c) go away snapped my sister irritably

_____

d) youre very welcome to stay said patrick

_____

e) thank you my aunt whispered

_____

70 Punctuate these sentences. (All are 'narrative first, speech second'.)

a) the prime minister said that question is out of order

_____

b) she cried very loudly you always pick on me

_____

c) mrs sandiford said theres no homework tonight

_____

d) dr grimes asked gently how long have you been feeling like this

_____

e) my mother yelled suppers ready

_____

71 Punctuate the sentences. (All are 'speech interrupted by narrative'.)

a) nobody he said firmly can understand that horror of imprisonment unless they have experienced it themselves

_____

_____

b) im sorry to disturb you the young woman said timidly but can you help me

_____

_____

c) i can assure my uncle said fervently that i was lucky to escape with my life

_____

_____

d) just go away shouted alan and leave me in peace

_____

_____

e) youll be very unpopular his wife warned when the twins find out about this

_____

_____

72 Punctuate these longer speeches.

a) our house said elaine has been on the market now for ten months only a handful of people have been to look round i think were going to have to reduce the asking price

_____

_____

_____

b) welcome to lascelles and company said eric our tour begins here in reception we move next to the original factory building where the keyboards are still assembled

_____

_____

_____

c) have you heard the news anna asked theyre going to change the national curriculum yet again when will it end

_____

_____

_____

d) matthew said i dont really feel like going out at all tonight i think ill have an early night

_____

_____

_____

e) whats the matter with you retorted his brother are you getting old before your time its only eight oclock

_____

_____

_____

73 There is one punctuation error in each of the sentences below. Circle it and write the correction in the space provided.

a) "Go away!" Cried Mrs Owen angrily. _____

b) "I'm sure there's been a dreadful mistake" said Brendan. _____

c) "Are you coming to London with us?" she asked? _____

d) He said, "We all want to help". _____

e) "It's a long story," said the woman in the red coat. "And I really don't know where to begin." _____

f) "Have a nice weekend," called Mary. _____

g) The policeman took out his notebook and said, "tell me exactly what happened."

_____

h) "I'd love to come" Brenda said, "but I can't afford to this month. Perhaps you'll invite me next time?" _____

i) "Do you want to drive"? asked Karl. _____

j) "Have a sweet," said Jimmy. "Thank you," said Tom. _____

Indirect speech

See how Michelle Magorian makes effective use of indirect speech in another extract from *Goodnight Mister Tom*:

> She'd been asking her mother for ages if she could wear shorts but had been told that she'd turn into a boy if she did and no man would want to marry her. Her father had said it was all right by him but he had already let her have her own way about the high school and didn't want to cause any more friction.

From *Goodnight Mister Tom* by Michelle Magorian (Puffin 1983)

A lot of talking over a considerable period of time has been condensed into this one paragraph. Indirect speech enables you in this way to 'get on with the story' when little would be gained by quoting what was said.

When you convert direct speech to indirect speech, you have to adjust:
- verb tenses
- pronouns
- possessive adjectives
- some references to time and place.

Tenses of verbs

Direct speech: "I am sorry," he said, "that I kicked your car."
Indirect speech: He said that he was sorry that he had kicked her car.

Everything is taken one stage further back in time:

Direct speech tenses		Indirect speech tenses
he kicks	⟶	he kicked
he is kicking	⟶	he was kicking
he does kick	⟶	he did kick
he kicked	⟶	he had kicked
he did kick	⟶	he had kicked
he has kicked	⟶	he had kicked
he has been kicking	⟶	he had been kicking
he will kick	⟶	he would kick
he will be kicking	⟶	he would be kicking
he will have kicked	⟶	he would have kicked
he will have been kicking	⟶	he would have been kicking

Pronouns

Direct speech: "Why did you do it?" she asked him.
Indirect speech: She asked him why he had done it.

Change all pronouns to the third person:

I, me; myself
you (sing.); yourself }➝ he, him; she, her; himself, herself

we, us; ourselves
you (pl.); yourselves }➝ they, them; themselves

Possessive adjectives

Direct speech: "I am sorry that I kicked your car," he said.
Indirect speech: He said that he was sorry he had kicked her car.

my, your (sing.)➝his/her
our, your (pl.)➝their

References to time and place

Direct speech: "I'll meet you here tomorrow," promised Shaun.
Indirect speech: Shaun promised that he would meet her there the next day.

now➝then
at this moment➝at that moment
today➝that day
yesterday➝the previous day, the day before
tomorrow➝the next day, the day after
here➝there
this place➝that place

...and so on

Note: The punctuation of indirect questions and indirect commands
When questions and commands are changed from direct to indirect speech, they become statements **and need full stops**.

"How are you?" he asked.➝He asked how she was.
"Stop talking!" she shouted.➝She ordered the class to stop talking.

Activities

74 Decide which of the following sentences are direct questions requiring question marks and which are indirect questions requiring full stops.

a) Would you like a sweet _____

b) I wonder if they have arrived yet _____

c) Can you drive _____

d) Simon asked her if she was feeling better _____

e) I don't know whether you are joking or not _____

f) Did Delia get her essay finished _____

g) She asked me if I could babysit _____

h) We asked the police for advice about security _____

i) Did you make them yourself _____

j) May I make a suggestion _____

75 Rewrite these examples of direct speech as indirect speech.

a) "I am delighted to be with you all today," said the Mayor.

The Mayor said that _____

_____

b) At 9.30 p.m., Bob suddenly remarked, "I'll be in London this time tomorrow."

At 9.30 p.m., Bob suddenly remarked that _____

_____

c) "You can come in now," said Olivia.

Olivia said that _____

d) "It's no joke bringing up a young family on a low income," Elsie Tavener said bitterly.

Elsie Tavener said bitterly that _____

_____

e) "I want to see the head teacher this minute. It's urgent!" insisted Mr Dunn.

Mr Dunn said that _____

and insisted that _____

76 Use your dictionary to help you establish the exact difference in meaning between:

a) to reply _____

    to retort _____

b) to ask _____

    to plead _____

c) to interrupt _____

    to interject _____

d) to repeat _____

    to reiterate _____

77

Read this extract from *Great Expectations* by Charles Dickens. It describes Pip's first meeting with Miss Havisham.

"Who is it" said the lady at the table.

"Pip, ma'am."

"Pip?"

"Mr pumblechook's boy, ma'am. Come – to play."

"Come nearer; let me look at you. Come close."

It was when I stood before her, avoiding her eyes, that I took note of the surounding objects in detail, and saw that her watch had stopped at twenty minutes to nine, and that a clock in the room had stopped at twenty minuites to nine.

"Look at me," said Miss Havisham "You are not affraid of a woman who has never seen the sun since you were born?"

I regret to state that I was not afraid of telling the enormous lie comprehended in the answer "No."

"Do you know what I touch here?" she said, laying her hands, one upon the other, on her left side.

"Yes, ma'am."

"What do I touch?"

"Your heart"

"Broken!"

She uttered the word with an eager look, and with strong emphasis, and with a wierd smile that had a kind of boast in it. Afterwards, she kept her hands there for a little while, and slowly took them away as if they were heavy.

"I am tiered" said Miss Havisham. "I want diversion, and I have done with men and women. Play."

From *Great Expectations* by Charles Dickens (Penguin 1965)

a) Circle the five spelling errors that have been deliberately introduced. Write corrections in the spaces provided.

b) Circle the five deliberate punctuation errors. Write the corrections in the spaces provided.

c) Why is there an apostrophe in 'Mr Pumblechook's boy'?

_____

d) Why is there an apostrophe in 'ma'am'?

_____

e) 'Come nearer; let me look at you.' How else could this be punctuated without using a semi-colon? _____

_____

f) What do you learn about Miss Havisham from the way she speaks?

_____

_____

g) Rewrite the first five lines of the extract as indirect speech.

_____

_____

_____

_____

_____

Paragraphing

What is a paragraph?

> A paragraph is a section in a piece of writing which deals with one main idea. It always begins on a new line. There is no set length.

Some pupils have been known to try to paragraph their work **after** it has been written. This is usually impossible because the ideas have all become so jumbled that they cannot be separated.

- It's always best to plan beforehand the points you want to make and establish the best order for them. Then paragraphing becomes straightforward.
- Start a new paragraph every time you move on to the next point. Make a point and develop it fully, and then move on again.
- Show where each paragraph begins either by indenting 2–3 cm from the left-hand margin or by leaving a clear line between each paragraph. Either method is fully acceptable but you should be consistent.

Well paragraphed writing is a courtesy to the reader. It enables the reader to follow without confusion your line of thought and to see at a glance the structure of the piece.

> Paragraphing is the visual presentation of the logical structure of a piece of writing.

Paragraph checklist

When you are checking through an important piece of writing, pay particular attention to paragraph structure and content.

PARAGRAPH CHECKLIST

- Is the main idea of each paragraph clear? ☐

- Is everything relevant? Should anything be omitted? ☐

- Is any paragraph overloaded? Should it really be two (or even three) paragraphs making related points? ☐

- Should anything be added to support the main idea in any of the paragraphs? (In a literature essay, for example, you will want to ensure that you've used quotations and references wisely in support of each point you make.) ☐

- Should the order of the paragraphs be rearranged? (You will sometimes find, for example, that your concluding paragraph makes a very good introduction.) ☐

- Does each paragraph lead easily to the next? Should any linking words and phrases be added? ☐

- Are the paragraph boundaries clearly indicated by indenting or spacing? ☐

Activities

78 Write a paragraph about one item of furniture in your bedroom. Everything you say must be strictly relevant to this one piece of furniture.

_____

_____

_____

_____

_____

_____

_____

_____

_____

_____

_____

_____

_____

_____

_____

_____

_____

79 Read the following extract from _Jobs and Careers After 'A' Levels_ and then answer the questions in exercise 80.

> Nonetheless in the present job situation it is very unlikely you will get the first job you try for, so do not narrow down your choice of employer too much. Applying for a job does not commit you to taking the job even if it is offered to you, so apply for as many jobs as take your interest. You should apply for them all at once. Don't wait for a rejection as a result of interview before trying the next job.
>
> Rejections are always discouraging but making the assumption that it is all hopeless and there is no point in trying to get a good job is certain to lead to expectations being fulfilled. Some students react to their first failure to get into, for example, a management training scheme, by assuming they will only be able to get a labourer's job. This too is inflicting unnecessary limitations on themselves. It is realistic to expect to have to make compromises but don't overreact to the difficulties.
>
> It's no help to escape from the problems of getting a job by 'drifting' into higher education. This could just be storing up worse problems for later on! It is also a mistake just to leave it all hoping that 'something will turn up', as it probably will not.

From _Jobs and Careers After 'A' Levels_ by Mary Munro (CRAC/Hobsons Publishing 1988)

30

a) Give a suitable title for the extract.

_____

b) Provide a heading for each paragraph.

Paragraph 1 _____

Paragraph 2 _____

Paragraph 3 _____

c) What general point is the example in paragraph 2 illustrating?

_____

d) Give a logical reason for the double letters in 'overreact' (para. 2).

_____

e) Supply the nouns formed from these verbs:

apply (para. 1) _____

commit (para. 1) _____

react (para. 2) _____

f) Find an example in the second paragraph of a noun that forms its plural other than by simply adding -s.

g) Give words opposite in meaning to these two words in the passage:

rejection (para. 1) _____

failure (para. 2) _____

h) Why is 'drifting' in paragraph 3 in inverted commas?

_____

_____

i) Why is 'something will turn up' in paragraph 3 in inverted commas?

j) Why does the first word of para. 3 have an apostrophe?

_____

_____

k) Find an example in the paragraph of an adverb and an adverbial clause.

adverb _____

adverbial clause _____

Topic sentences

Sometimes the central idea of a paragraph will be implied; sometimes it will be clearly stated in a sentence within the paragraph.

> A sentence which sums up the main idea in a paragraph is called the **topic sentence.**

In your reading you will find that if a writer uses a topic sentence it is often the very first sentence in the paragraph. The idea is then developed (and perhaps illustrated by examples) in the rest of the paragraph.

Occasionally, the topic sentence (if there is one) is delayed until later in the paragraph or even kept as a climax until the very end.

You might like to experiment in your own writing with the use of a topic sentence and with the impact gained by varying its position.

Let us look at four examples.

Paragraph A

In this example, the topic of this short paragraph is perfectly clear and there is no topic sentence.

> The castle lavatories or garderobes were generally set in small rooms built into the thick outside walls. They were reached down a short passage, so that they were apart from the living quarters. Usually there were some on each floor. There was a simple stone seat, and sewage went down a chute on the exterior wall into the moat or a convenient river or into a pit at the base of the wall.

From *Castles: A Guide for Young People* (Macmillan/HMSO 1977, for the Department of the Environment)

Paragraph B

This example shows how effective it can be to start a paragraph with a topic sentence which will sum up all the details that follow.

You can do anything on a right of way that is 'reasonably incidental' to your journey. This is largely a matter of common sense. You can carry a bag or backpack, for example, and wheel a pushchair if it is practical to do so. You can stop for a rest, to admire the view or take a photograph, or sit down to eat a simple picnic. But you should not camp or light a fire without getting permission from the landowner. Nor should you deliberately disturb people or animals or misuse the path in any way. On one occasion, a person who misused a right of way by shouting and waving flags to disrupt a shooting party was found by the court to have been trespassing. So was a racing tipster who used a path to make notes on racehorses training near by.

From *Enjoying the Northern Ireland Countryside* (Department of Environment for Northern Ireland)

Paragraph C

This example shows how it can be useful to delay the topic sentence until after an introduction. This paragraph is taken from a speech in the House of Commons. Formal speech has a paragraph structure too as points are made, one by one.

Ms Morris: I shall start by saying something that will find agreement on both sides of the House on the importance of literacy in teaching and learning. **It is important to master that basic skill if one is to access the rest of the curriculum and to realise one's potential.** It is true to say that literacy, more than any other subject, underpins everyone's learning. Certainly, in the debate we had on this issue in Committee, the Minister made clear his agreement with us that any measures that would help to raise literacy standards in our schools should be considered.

From *Hansard*, Column 176, 28 January 1997

Paragraph D

And, finally, we have an example of the topic sentence being delayed for maximum effect until the very end of the paragraph. (You will gather that Col. John Mohune is also known as Blackbeard.)

Now when I saw that, I felt a sort of throttling fright, as though one had caught hold of my heartstrings; and so many and such strange thoughts rose in me, that the blood went pounding round and round in my head, as it did once afterwards when I was fighting with the sea and near drowned. Surely to have in hand the beard of any dead man in any place was bad enough, but worse a thousand times in such a place as this, and to know on whose face it had grown. **For, almost before I fully saw what it was, I knew it was that black beard which had given Colonel John Mohune his nickname, and this was his great coffin I had hid behind.**

From *Moonfleet* by J. Meade Falkner (1898)

Activities

81 Underline the topic sentence in each of these paragraphs.

a) First impressions count, especially when it comes to selling your home. Prospective buyers may have a whole series of properties to view and will make comparisons as they go along. If you have accentuated all your home's finer points and have it and your garden in top shape, you will guarantee that whoever comes to view it will walk away with a positive impression.

From 'Selling your home' by Mary O'Connor in *Western People*, Ballina, Ireland, 11 June 1997

b) Back in England, the girls found themselves caught up in a round of parties. It was hard to remember God's call when the London season was in full swing. Parthe could think of nothing but enjoying herself, and the sisters were constantly surrounded by groups of charming young men, in tight trousers, and gay waistcoats, with twirling moustaches. Many of them fell in love with Florence at first sight, for she was always pointed out as the prettiest girl in the room. Queen Victoria's wedding to the handsome, serious young German, Prince Albert, filled London with people, and the Nightingales were invited everywhere, even to parties and receptions where the young Queen and her husband were also guests. Life could not have been more exciting.

From *Lady With a Lamp* by Cyril Davey (Lutterworth Press 1956)

c) He would do anything to produce better vegetables. Whenever a circus came near us, he used to go along with this pushcart which he'd made himself and collect elephant dung. Then he'd wheel it back along the High Street piled high with the stuff. It used to smell like nothing on earth. He didn't care, anything for his blessed allotment.

From 'Fashion' by Brian Keaney in *Autobiography* by John Foster (Oxford University Press 1991), reprinted from the *Don't Hang About* collection of short stories (Oxford University Press)

d) Louis Braille was born in northern France. He was blinded when he was three years old. His father was a saddler and the little boy loved to watch him work. One day, Louis crept into the workshop and tried to cut some leather by himself. The sharp knife slipped and stabbed him in the left eye. Both his eyes became infected and within a few months he was blind.

From *Twenty Inventors* by Jacqueline Dineau (Wayland 1988)

e) Another subject which I really feel confused about is equal rights. At school I am taught to believe that women are no less than men and they must have the chance of having equal opportunities; but at home, I am witnessing the fact that women are always being put down. We Nepalese girls are taught to respect the menfolk, because they have the knowledge and capability of doing everything. We are told that women are the weaker sex. Women must always stand by their husbands, whether they are right or wrong. Back in Nepal, the two words 'equal opportunities' would not even be heard of, let alone practised!

From 'Life for a young Asian girl' by Sangita Manandhar in *Autobiography* by John Foster (Oxford University Press 1991), reprinted from *Say What You Think* (The English and Media Centre)

32 From your own reading or from your own writing, find examples of:

a) a topic sentence coming first in a paragraph

b) a topic sentence coming last in a paragraph

c) a topic sentence coming other than first or last in a paragraph.

33 Rewrite these sentences in a logical order. There is no topic sentence.

a) It may be of loose snow, when the avalanche starts at a single point or a Slab Avalanche which occurs when an area of more cohesive snow separates from the surrounding snow and slides out.

b) These layers may have dissimilar physical properties.

c) An avalanche may be dry or wet, according to whether free water is present in the snow.

d) Snow is deposited in successive layers as winter progresses.

e) An avalanche occurs when one layer slides on another, or the whole snow cover slides on the ground.

From *This Leaflet Could Stop an Avalanche* (The Scottish Mountain Safety Group/The Scottish Sports Council)

_____

_____

_____

_____

_____

_____

_____

_____

_____

_____

_____

34 Supply a topic sentence for this paragraph and indicate with an arrow where you would place it in the paragraph.

Circuses may travel hundreds of miles a year and the animals are transported in cages or beast wagons which invariably become the animals' home. The available space is often less than 2.5 square metres per lion, tiger or leopard.

From *Don't Go to the Circus* (RSPCA 1997)

_____

_____

_____

Planning an essay

Some essays are much more straightforward to write than others but all involve a certain amount of selection and shaping of material.

> Planning an essay means collecting your material and sorting it into a logical sequence **before** you start writing.

Collecting your material

After studying the essay title carefully, it's worth jotting down **everything** that comes immediately to mind. Don't reject anything at this stage. This 'brainstorming' will encourage ideas to come thick and fast, and you will find that one idea will trigger another.

Focus intently. Give your whole mind to what you want to say, why you want to say it, and what response you want to evoke in your reader.

If you're setting out to describe something you remember vividly, tap all the senses and list memorable sights, smells, tastes, sounds, textures and movements; if you're planning to defend a point of view, then explore sincerely all the reasons you feel passionately about the subject and try to anticipate all the counter-arguments that could be made.

Finally, make sure that you've not left any important avenue unexplored by checking who? what? why? when? where? how? against the title. Some answers to these questions may suggest additional paragraphs.

If your subject is 'Dreams', for example, there's a great deal of material in **who** dreams? **what** are dreams? **why** do we dream? **when** do we dream? **where** do we dream? **how** do we dream? and even, **what if** we didn't or couldn't dream?

Use this series of questions too at the beginning, if your mind is a total blank.

Sorting your material

Once you've collected all your material together, take a long critical look at it. It's unlikely that you'll keep it all. Group all the related points under different headings and see what the paragraph topics could be.

Then arrange the topics themselves in the best possible order. Some subjects will lend themselves to a chronological approach (an account of a school trip, for example), but other more discursive essays will need careful organising.

Experiment a little with the paragraph sequence and spend some time selecting a good beginning and a satisfactory way of ending the essay.

One way of beginning an essay is to use a relevant statistic or quotation or an intriguing statement. On the other hand, a simple summary of what is to come can be equally effective.

A concluding paragraph that rounds the essay off satisfactorily is vital. Don't come to a sudden halt or give the impression that you've run out of ideas. A conclusion doesn't have to be elaborate. A simple sentence summing up your line of thought in the essay can often be enough.

Activities

85 Below are some essay titles and some possible paragraph topics. Arrange the topics in a logical order.

a) The Play

– ticket sales	i	_____
– dress rehearsal	ii	_____
– auditions	iii	_____
– first night	iv	_____
– reviews	v	_____
– rehearsals	vi	_____

b) Stratford Outing

– waiting for latecomers	i	_____
– picnic lunch by river	ii	_____
– late arrival in Stratford	iii	_____
– waiting at stage door	iv	_____
– coach journey home	v	_____
– performance	vi	_____
– early morning register	vii	_____

c) The Driving Test

– alone with the examiner	i	_____
– arrival at the test centre	ii	_____
– mistakes made during test	iii	_____
– waiting for the examiner	iv	_____
– the result	v	_____
– the last practice lesson	vi	_____
– the night before the test	vii	_____

86 Write the introductory paragraph for an essay entitled: 'My grandfather'.

_____

_____

_____

_____

_____

_____

_____

_____

_____

37

Read this newspaper article and decide how each paragraph contributes to the overall plan. Briefly summarise the topic of each paragraph in the space provided.

Angela Goad peered out of her window on to Godstone's pretty village green and saw a class of children wandering around with clipboards. How sweet, she thought.

Over the months, more pupils appeared on day trips, investigating the common, looking at the historic Surrey village's buildings and visiting the church, scribbling answers to their questions as they went. Numbers began to creep up. Sometimes the doughty district councillor saw two coaches arrive on the same day, sometimes three. Then this summer, when the weather improved, things started to get out of hand. Half a dozen coaches turned up most days – 14 on one June morning, delivering close to 700 pupils to a village with no coach park, no shelter from rain, only one set of public toilets, and elderly residents who like children, but...not quite so many.

And some children, frankly, were out of control. In the sheltered flats of the converted alms house by the church, residents watched horrified as children peered through their windows or played hopscotch on the conveniently laid-out square of cremation plaques in the graveyard next door.

Why had Godstone become such an attraction? Parish council clerk Pat Rodgers uncovered the answer: *Discover Godstone*, an award-winning resource pack complete with historic and recent photographs designed to help primary schools to teach history and geography. Every teacher in driving distance was apparently taking the title literally.

It could make an interesting national curriculum topic. Investigate how many coachloads of children it takes to really, *really*, annoy a village. How long does it take 600 pupils to queue for just six toilets? How many bags of rubbish can a school outing create in a morning? Perhaps someone should write a teaching pack...

Adapted from 'The hell of Godstone village' by Nicolas Barnard in *The Times Educational Supplement*, 27 June 1997

Paragraph 1

_____

_____

_____

Paragraph 2

_____

_____

_____

Paragraph 3

_____

_____

_____

Paragraph 4

_____

_____

_____

Paragraph 5

_____

_____

_____

Drafting, redrafting and proofreading

Drafting

All writers draft and redraft their work. When you come to apply for a job or a college place, you'll find you'll probably spend at least one evening perfecting your application.

When it comes to writing an important essay assignment, you'll want to take time to make it as perfect as you can.

Writing the first draft

Concentrate on getting down all that you want to say and making it as vivid and interesting as you can. Communicate your enthusiasm. Write sincerely. Focus on the task in hand.

Don't worry at this stage about looking up spellings. These can be checked at the proofreading stage and so can any punctuation points.

Writing the second draft

Read your first draft critically. Have you always made your meaning clear? Do you need to expand any points or add more details? Is everything relevant? Should anything be omitted?

Read your work aloud if possible. How does it sound? Have you expressed yourself clumsily at any point? Go over what you have written again and again, improving your sentence construction, finding just the right word, removing any slang or pompous expressions that may have slipped in. Look critically at the paragraphing. Make the introductory paragraph and the conclusion as effective as you can.

Don't be surprised if you make several drafts before you're satisfied.

Here's an example of some redrafted work for one of the paragraphs above. I find it useful to use a different coloured pen for alterations and corrections.

> Concentrate on getting down all that you want to say and ~~getting the right tone for your audience~~ making it as vivid and interesting as you can. Communicate your ~~involvement with the subject and your~~ enthusiasm. Write sincerely. ~~Take trouble.~~ Focus on the task in hand. Don't worry at this stage about looking up spellings. ~~Underline any words you intend to check later.~~ These can be checked at the proofreading stage and so can any punctuation points.

Proofreading

Proofreading means reading your work very carefully at the end so that spelling, punctuation and grammar mistakes can be corrected.

PROOFREADING CHECKLIST

- Now is the time to check the spelling of any words you're uncertain about. Look particularly carefully at any words that usually cause you difficulty. ☐

- Check the punctuation carefully, sentence by sentence. Make sure you've used full stops, question marks or exclamation marks where sentences end and **not** commas. Check apostrophes, capital letters and all the places where commas should be used. If you've used direct speech, check you have made no errors. ☐

- Check tenses and agreement between subject and verb. ☐

- Check that you have made no other grammatical slips. ☐

- Check that no words have been missed out accidentally. ☐

Your essay should now be as good as you can make it.

Well done!

Activities

88 The sentences below are ridiculously pompous. Rewrite them more simply using the number of words indicated in the brackets.

a) Permit me to express my warmest felicitations on your recent betrothal. (4)

_____

b) The fourteenth anniversary of my natal day is fast approaching. (5)

_____

c) The diminution in the effectiveness of my ocular organs has necessitated the employment of optical aids. (5)

_____

d) Their endeavours to extinguish the conflagration were futile. (7)

_____

e) Trevor must not desist from his endeavours to ameliorate his penmanship. (5)

_____

89 Can you see what is clumsy stylistically in this sentence?

He didn't **return back** until midnight.

The word 'back' is not needed as 'return' **means** 'come back'.

Rewrite these sentences, pruned of unnecessary repetition.

a) She told me her address and then repeated it again as I wrote it down.

_____
_____

b) Stephen looked very handsome as he left the church with the bride he had married on his arm.

_____
_____

c) The workforce all agreed unanimously that they would take a reduction in wages to help keep the firm afloat.

_____
_____

d) I think he should be forcibly compelled to reimburse you.

_____
_____

e) She could see the chaos with her own eyes.

_____
_____

f) If you want, why not volunteer to help?

_____

_____

g) He was an only child and had no brothers and sisters.

_____

_____

h) Both parents were killed in a fatal car accident.

_____

_____

i) If you're not careful, that infection could recur again.

_____

_____

j) Jane is one of those reliable people who always arrive punctually on time.

_____

_____

90 Choose the right word.

a) Wheat, rye, maize and barley are all _____ crops. (cereal/serial)

b) Adam paid for the petrol by _____. (check/cheque)

c) Of _____, we're only joking. (coarse/course)

d) Tabitha stood as an independent candidate in the last _____ election. (council/counsel)

e) We must do something about the _____ under the front door. (draft/draught)

f) Tim was told in no uncertain terms not to _____ with what did not concern him. (medal/meddle)

g) Make sure that you _____ the date at the top of each assignment. (right/write)

h) Bonita and Geraldine now _____ much happier. (seam/seem)

i) We've just discovered that the school is on the _____ of a Roman Villa. (sight/site)

j) Unfortunately, they _____ the ball with such force that it broke a street lamp. (threw/through)

Writing in different genres

genre (*noun*): a type, kind, class of composition...

You will probably already have had experience of writing in a wide range of genres. You may have written, in addition to essays of different kinds:

poems

playscripts

letters

diary entries

simple report

stories for young children

factual accounts

book reviews

newspaper articles.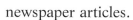

In addition, you will almost certainly have read an even wider range:

leaflets

recipes

brochures

magazine articles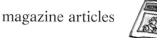

instruction manuals

obituaries

posters

invitations

notices

questionnaires

advertisements

You may also have seen:
official forms
legal documents
minutes
formal reports

prospectuses
agendas
memoranda
business letters.

The list of genres is almost endless. If you want to compile a really useful reference file, you could try to collect one good example of each of the genres listed above.

Each genre has its own particular conventions of presentation, style and tone.

You need to be alert to these conventions if you are to write convincingly and effectively within these genres.

Presentation and meaning

If you have access to a word processor, you will be able to experiment with different fonts and should be able to present leaflets, invitations, advertisements, newspaper articles, posters and notices very effectively by taking advantage of the different visual possibilities available. Much is possible, of course, in longhand.

See how the designer has made the cover of this leaflet eye-catching:

From *Litter and the Law*
(Tidy Northern Ireland)

In a different style, this advertisement is equally eye-catching. You might like to calculate how many different kinds of lettering have been used and the number of colours.

From *The Beano*, 14 June 1997
(© D. C. Thomson & Co. Ltd 1997)

Activities

91 Design an advertisement to fit the box below, using all the details provided (but correct any spelling, punctuation and grammar errors!).

Anual Craft Fair Emmanuel Church Tower Street Official Openning 2.30 p.m. by the Lord Mayer Saterday 6 December Every one are very wellcome

92 What important information has been omitted from this memo?

```
                         MEMORANDUM
From:        Alex Douglas, Sales Manager
To:          Sales Representatives in the UK
Date:        26 November 1998
Subject:     Quality Control at Erith Factory
There will be a meeting to discuss quality control at the new
factory. All Sales Representatives are required to attend. It
will begin at 10 a.m. and will be held at the Imperial Hotel,
Birmingham.
```

Alex Douglas has not included the _____.

93 Read 'Spice Crisis'.

SPICE CRISIS

Hit writers dumped

The Spice Girls are locked in crisis talks with their record company as their multi-million pound empire is on the brink of collapse.

In the latest blow, it was revealed the writers behind their smash-hit songs are no longer signed to them.

The music men who helped write their best-selling singles are contracted to their sacked management company – not the band.

Yesterday, the stars were holding emergency talks with Virgin record bosses.

They have been left without their army of support staff after dumping their guru Simon Fuller and his company 19 Management.

But music business insiders said losing their top song writers would be the biggest hurdle for the girls to overcome.

Credits

Richard Stannard and Matt Rowe have been the brains behind a string of their number ones.

They co-wrote Wanna-bee, Say You'll Be There and Two Become One and other tracks.

Although the girls get song-writing credits, insiders say the two men have come up with the heart of their hits.

An insider said: "Stannard and Rowe have been responsible for the girls' biggest successes.

"Although the Spice Girls have helped write them the pair are the real brains behind their multi-million selling hits.

"Unless the band have good material even the cleverest promotion will not keep them at the top." ■

From *The Star*, 12 November 1997, page 14

a) What makes the title eyecatching? (Mention as many factors as you can.)

_____

_____

_____

_____

_____

_____

_____

b) What is the function of the subheadings?

_____

_____

_____

c) Why do you think the paragraphs are so short?

_____

_____

_____

d) How many sentences are there on average in a paragraph? _____

e) Which paragraph virtually repeats the information given in the opening paragraph?

_____

f) Why have paragraphs five and nine been singled out for particular attention?

_____

_____

_____

_____

The informal friendly letter

Use either the traditional or the fully blocked layout. Both are fully acceptable, but you shouldn't mix the two forms.

Traditional layout

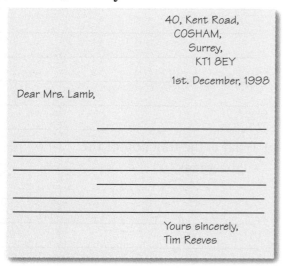

- address slopes at 45°
- paragraphs are indented
- complimentary close and signature bottom right
- punctuation above and below body of letter

Optional

- comma after house number
- full stop at end of line before postcode
- full stop after 1st and Mrs

Fully blocked layout

- address is blocked
- paragraphs are blocked and not indented
- clear space left between paragraphs
- open punctuation (no commas or full stops above or below body of letter)
- complimentary close and signature bottom left

Optional

- writer's address on left of page
- date on left of page

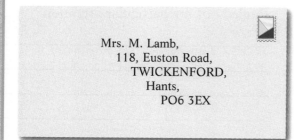

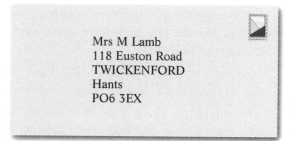

The formal business letter

Use either the traditional or the fully blocked layout, but don't mix the two.

Traditional layout

```
                          3, Fir Lane,
                          BOLEYARD,
                          Essex,
                          LT5 2NF

                          2nd. May, 1999
The Editor,
'The Clarion',
Key Road,
NATCHAM,
LT6 8EB

Dear Sir,

     _____

_____
_____
_____
_____
_____
_____
_____
_____

                          Yours faithfully,
                          Emma Carter
```

Fully blocked layout

```
                          3 Fir Lane
                          BOLEYARD
                          Essex
                          LT5 2NF

                          2 May 1999
The Editor
The Clarion
Key Road
NATCHAM
LT6 8EB

Dear Sir,

_____
_____
_____
_____

_____
_____

_____
_____

Yours faithfully
Emma Carter
```

- writer's address slopes at 45° top right
- line left between writer's address and date
- another line left between date and address of recipient on left
- address of recipient against straight 'margin'
- paragraphs indented
- complimentary close and signature bottom right
- punctuation above and below body of letter

Optional
- comma after house number
- full stop at end of line before postcode
- full stop after 2nd

- both addresses blocked
- paragraphs blocked and not indented
- clear space left between paragraphs
- open punctuation (no commas or full stops above or below body of letter)
- complimentary close and signature bottom left

Optional
- writer's address on left of page
- date on left of page

Activities

There are punctuation, spelling, grammar and presentational errors in this traditionally laid-out formal letter of application for a job.

Circle each error and write corrections in the spaces provided.

14 New avenue,

Exford,

Somerset

TA29EY

21.7.99

The Personnel Officer,

Optics Ltd.,

Weybridge Estate,

Didbury, TA4 3QY

Dear Sir or Madame

     I was very intrested to read in yesterdays Somerset Clarion that theres a vacancy for a trainee design technitian with Optics Ltd. i should very much to be considered for the post.

     I have six GCSE passes at Grade C and above as you will see from the CV i enclose i gained Grade C in mathmatics and english and Grade A in art.

     I have allways enjoy Art and Design and the oppertunity to work in the design department appealls to me very much. Last summer when i were in Year 10 i done my work experience at Optics and i enjoied it very much.

     I should wellcome the chance of day release at Didbury College while working at Optics.

     I hope very much you will consider me for the post i can come for interveiw at eny time.

Your's Faithfuly

Anita Gibson

_____
_____
_____
_____
_____
_____
_____
_____
_____
_____
_____
_____
_____
_____
_____
_____
_____
_____
_____
_____
_____
_____
_____

95 Write out the corrected letter opposite in fully blocked layout.

Style and tone

Remember that each item within each genre will have been written for a particular purpose and with a particular audience in mind.

> Language, style and tone must be appropriate to purpose and audience.

Notice how the writers' awareness of purpose and audience has influenced the language, style and tone of these extracts.

> Once there was a boy who worked for a king. But the king was cruel to him. So the boy ran away. He met a big lion in the desert. The boy was afraid because the lion looked angry.

From *The Boy and the Lion* by Val Biro (Ginn 1983) – for readers aged 5½–6½

- simple words often of one syllable
- short sentences and simple statements
- repetition of key words for reading practice
- intention to provide action story that a small child can read independently

> Hi Rach!
>
> I'm having a party and sleepover next Saturday. Can you come? It starts at 6 pm and there'll be loads of grub (plus your favourite crisps!). I've got Back Street Boys Live in America for us to watch. What do you reckon? We can have a major gossip all night!
>
> See ya!
>
> Anna

An invitation from 14-year-old girl to a friend

- slang (grub, major) and colloquialisms (loads of, reckon)
- contractions (I'm, there'll, I've, we'll)
- exclamation marks everywhere to reflect excitement
- deliberate misspelling (see ya!) to look 'cool'
- intention to write conversationally to a close friend

> We shall go on to the end. We shall fight in France. We shall fight on the seas and oceans. We shall fight with growing confidence and growing strength in the air. We shall defend our island, whatever the cost may be. We shall fight on the beaches. We shall fight on the landing grounds. We shall fight in the fields and in the streets. We shall fight in the hills. We shall never surrender.

From Winston Churchill's broadcast speech to the nation, June 1940, reprinted from *Great War Speeches* by Winston Churchill (Corgi Books 1957)

- use of 'we' to include whole nation
- repetition of 'we shall fight' to convey determination
- repetitive sentence structure builds up to climax
- balanced phrases 'in the...in the...', 'on the...on the...', 'growing...and growing...' suggests calmness
- intention to stir the listening public to patriotic fervour and to inspire confidence in leadership (spoken aloud in the Churchillian voice with impressive pauses even more effective!)

> This certificate is issued in pursuance of section 65 of the Marriage Act 1949. Sub-section 3 of this section provides that any certified copy of entry purporting to be sealed or stamped with the seal of the General Register Office shall be received as evidence of the marriage to which it relates without any further or other proof of the entry, and no certified copy purporting to have been given in the said Office shall be of any force or effect unless it is sealed or stamped as aforesaid.

From a 'Certified Copy of an Entry of Marriage', issued by the General Register Office in 1996. From The Office for National Statistics. Crown copyright is reproduced with the permission of the Controller of Her Majesty's Stationery Office.

- use of precise 'legal' language ('without any **further** or **other** proof'; 'shall be of any **force** or **effect**')
- use of archaic phrases ('aforesaid', 'in pursuance of')
- use of passive constructions ('this certificate **is issued**', '**shall be received**', '**to have been given**')
- very long second sentence which aims to close every loophole.
- intention is to clarify legal position unambiguously (and to sound suitably solemn in the process!)

Activities

96 Read these extracts carefully and identify genre, purpose and targeted audience.

a) People's President Mary McAleese cast aside the pomp and ceremony of her inauguration yesterday – and found out what it's like to be a pop star.

She invited 800 school kids to her big day and after the official part of the ceremonies at Dublin Castle was complete, she shook hands with almost every single one of them.

Genre _____

Purpose _____

Audience _____

b) There's nothing like the pleasure of choosing a good book and Book Tokens are the only vouchers you can buy and exchange in virtually every bookshop in the country. You can give exactly the value you want, as Book Tokens start at £1 and go up to £20. And now you can choose from a range of free colourful presentation wallets with their own detachable bookmarks.

Genre _____

Purpose _____

Audience _____

c) A number of different species of native plants can be found as troublesome weeds in lawns. These can be dug up individually or dealt with by applying a weedkiller. See *Pests and Diseases: Herbicides*.

Genre _____

Purpose _____

Audience _____

d) For the rest of her time in the Crimea Florence worked less in the hospitals, which were now well organised, and more in trying to help the soldiers in their spare time. She had the beer-shops closed, and opened schools and coffee-houses instead. She worked out a way in which soldiers could send money home to their families. She proved that if they were given a chance, soldiers were not the dirty, dishonest, drunken creatures they were often supposed to be, but good, clean, respectable men.

Genre _____

Purpose _____

Audience _____

e) To get the best out of your PCW 9512+, you must make sure that it is kept away from all extremes of temperature. In addition, the discs must be kept away from sources of magnetism such as telephones.

Genre _____

Purpose _____

Audience _____

97 Choose any one of the extracts in exercise 96, and comment on any features of style and tone that you feel to be appropriate for its purpose and targeted audience.

_____

_____

_____

_____

_____

_____

_____

_____

_____

_____

_____

_____

_____

_____

_____

_____

_____

_____

_____

_____

_____

_____

_____

_____

_____

_____

_____

_____

_____

_____

_____

_____

_____

_____

Activities

98 Rewrite these sentences in Standard English, avoiding all slang and colloquialisms.

a) Trevor spends all his dosh on booze and fags.

_____

b) I'm really fed up. Our car has conked out again.

_____

c) You must be round the bend if you think I would nick your coursework folder.

_____

d) Romeo fancied Juliet from the moment he eyed her up.

_____

e) When I was a kid, I thought twenty quid was a fortune.

_____

99 Rewrite these sentences, converting all the **bold** constructions to the passive voice.

a) If, after **sending me your Tax Return**, you find that **you have made a mistake**, let me know at once.

_____
_____

b) **Subtract the figure in box W55** from the figure in box W52 and **put the result** in box W56. **Put the figure** in brackets if the figure is negative.

_____
_____
_____

100 Rewrite these sentences, converting all the **bold** constructions to the active voice.

a) **You will only be penalised** if your Tax Return is incorrect through fraud or negligence.

_____
_____

b) The notes **are numbered** to match the boxes in your Tax Return.

_____
_____

Sentences in exercises 99 and 100 are from _Tax Return Guide_ and _Tax Calculation Guide_ (Inland Revenue/The Stationery Office, 1996)

Read the passage and answer the questions.

> And then, a few moments later, something happened; something so slight and so ordinary that afterwards Justin wondered if he had simply let his imagination run away with him – and yet he could never quite forget it, nor the sudden sense of evil that came with it. Roused perhaps by the warmth rising from the lamps, a big, soft-winged night-moth had come fluttering down from the rafters to dart and hover and swerve about the table. Everyone's attention was turned towards the Emperor, who was at that moment preparing to pour the second Libation to the gods. Everyone, that is, save Justin and Allectus. For some unknown reason, Justin had glanced again at Allectus; and Allectus was watching the moth.

From *The Silver Branch* by Rosemary Sutcliffe (Oxford University Press 1979)

a) Rewrite the first sentence of the passage in the 1st person (that is, using 'I' instead of 'he' and so on).

_____
_____
_____
_____
_____
_____

b) What does this passage gain or lose by being written in the 3rd person?

_____
_____
_____
_____
_____
_____

c) What makes the last sentence of the passage so effective?

_____
_____
_____
_____
_____
_____

d) This is an extract from an historical novel. How has this influenced the language and style?

_____
_____
_____
_____
_____

Practice assignments in different genres

102 **Advertisement**

Your school is to hold a fête to raise funds for the library. Devise a suitable advertisement for inclusion in your local newspaper.

103 **Account**

You have witnessed an accident between a car and a motor-cycle. Write an account for the police of exactly what you saw. Draw a map to support your account.

104 **Announcement**

New gas pipes are being laid under your school field. The school field will be out-of-bounds all week. Write the text for your headteacher's announcement.

105 **Brochure**

Your school is to be the venue for an activities holiday for two weeks in the summer. Devise a brochure detailing all the activities. Include a booking form.

106 **Conversation**

Write a conversation between two neighbours about your family.

107 **Diary entry**

Impersonate a character from a book you are reading at present and write a series of diary entries about events in the book.

108 **Essay (autobiographical)**

Write about a really happy or unhappy time in your life.

109 **Essay (descriptive)**

Write a vivid description of someone you know well.

110 **Essay (narrative)**

Write a short story in which this sentence is used: 'It is all my fault'.

111 **Essay (discursive)**

'It is a good time to be young.' Do you agree? Explain your views.

112 **Instructions**

A friend has offered to look after your pet while you are away. Write clear instructions on what should (and should not) be done.

113 **Invitation**

Devise and set out clearly a formal wedding invitation on behalf of two friends who are getting married.

114 Leaflet

Devise a leaflet outlining the school rules.

115 Letter (informal/friendly)

Write a letter to a friend who moved away from your area a month ago.

116 Letter (formal/business)

Write a letter to the editor of your local newspaper in reply to any letter recently published on its Letters page. (Set your letter out correctly even though it will appear in an abridged form when printed.)

117 Magazine article

Write an article for your school magazine about a school outing you enjoyed.

118 Newspaper article

Your school was totally destroyed by fire at the weekend. Write the report that appeared in your local evening paper the following Monday.

119 Obituary

Imagine that you have achieved all your ambitions in life. You die at 78. You are very famous. Write your obituary.

120 Playscript

Write a scene where parents meet their daughter's boyfriend for the first time. (Set it out like a scene in a play.)

121 Postcards

You are on holiday with your family. Write three postcards: one to your best friend; one to a relation; one to your English teacher.

122 Poster

Devise a poster advertising a school disco.

123 Questionnaire

Your school is conducting a survey into homework (how much time is spent each night, under what conditions is it done, how supportive families are, etc.) Devise an appropriate questionnaire.

124 Report

Write a report based on the findings of the questionnaire above, with recommendations for future action.

125 Review

Write a review of a book which you have thoroughly enjoyed recently and would recommend.

APPENDIX

Common grammatical errors

Among/between

Traditionally, the rule is that you use **between** when referring to two people and **among** when referring to three or more:

> Share the sweets between the two of you.

> Share the sweets among you all.

However, in some situations **between** is used instead of **among**:

> There is now agreement between the twelve companies concerned.

Be observant as you read and notice how these two prepositions are used in different contexts.

Agreement: singular and plural (adjectives, nouns and pronouns)

Remember that if you use a singular noun or pronoun any subsequent references must be singular. Similarly, if you use a plural noun or pronoun, subsequent references must be consistently plural:

- ✗ The effect on **the pupil** concerned would be disastrous if *they* felt isolated from all *their* friends.

- ✔ The effect on **the pupil** concerned would be disastrous if *he* felt isolated from all *his* friends.

- ✔ The effect on **the pupil** concerned would be disastrous if *she* felt isolated from all *her* friends.

- ✔ The effect on **the pupils** concerned would be disastrous if *they* felt isolated from all *their* friends.

Agreement: singular and plural (subject and verb)

Take care to match singular subjects with singular verbs and plural subjects with plural verbs:

- ✔ **The decision** *was* unanimous. (singular)

- ✔ The baby's **cries** *were* heard in the street. (plural)

Be particularly careful with double subjects and with constructions where it is easy to lose sight of the subject:

- ✔ **You and I** *are going* together. (plural)

- ✔ **Her intelligence and wit** *are admired* by all. (plural)

- ✔ **The huge selection** of study aids *is confusing*. (singular)

- ✔ **A swarm** of bees *was making* straight for us. (singular)

As/like

Use **as if** or **as though** to introduce a clause:

> You look **as if**/**as though** you have seen a ghost.

Use **like** with nouns and pronouns:

> You look **like** your father.

Comparison of adjectives

There are two ways of forming the comparative and the superlative of adjectives:

> short words: wide→wid**er**→wid**est**

> long words: beautiful→**more** beautiful→**most** beautiful

Don't mix the two methods!

> ✘ more wider

> ✘ most beautifullest

Comparison of adverbs

There are two ways of forming the comparative and the superlative of adverbs:

> monosyllables: fast→fast**er**→fast**est**

> longer words: neatly→**more** neatly→**most** neatly

Don't mix the two methods!

> ✘ more neatlier

> ✘ most fastest

Could of INCORRECT

Do not write **could of**, **should of**, **would of**, **might of**, **must of**. These are misspellings of the contracted forms.

Full form	Contracted form	Incorrect form
I could have	I could've	I could of
I should have	I should've	I should of
I would have	I would've	I would of
I might have	I might've	I might of
I must have	I must've	I must of

Due to/owing to

Use **due to** with nouns:

> Long **delays** *due to* fog are inevitable.

Use **owing to** with verbs:

> We **missed** the train *owing to* fog.

Either...or/neither...nor

Each word in the pair must be positioned carefully:

  ✗ I was advised either to consider nursing or social work.

  ✗ She neither can sing nor dance.

  ✔ I was advised to consider *either* nursing *or* social work.

  ✔ She can *neither* sing *nor* dance.

Fewer/less

Use **fewer** with nouns that can be counted.
Use **less** with nouns that can't be counted.

  Eat *fewer* biscuits.

  Eat *less* fat.

I/me

The difficulty usually arises with double subjects and double objects:

  You and _____ must decide. (I or me?)

  They have invited Ben and _____. (I or me?)

Recast the sentence mentally and the choice becomes clear:

  You must decide and **I** must decide. ➡You and **I** must decide.

  They have invited Ben and they have invited **me**. ➡They have invited Ben and **me**.

To lie/to lay

To lie (down)

  I **lie** down every afternoon.

  I **lay** down yesterday afternoon.

  I **have lain** down every afternoon this week.

To (tell a) lie

  I **lie** whenever I can.

  I **lied** yesterday.

  I **have lied** all my life.

To lay

  I **lay** the table every day.

  I **laid** the table yesterday.

  I **have laid** the table.

  The hen **lays** an egg.

  The hen **laid** five eggs.

  The hen **has laid** an egg.

Misrelated participles

The present participle ends in **-ing**.

The regular past participle ends in **-ed**.

Always be alert to possible ambiguity when you use participles as adjectives:

> ✗ **Walking** unsteadily across the road, the **glass** was shattered when Ian stumbled. (Who was walking unsteadily? The glass?)

> ✗ **Simmered** gently for half an hour, the whole **family** will enjoy stuffed peppers. (What was simmered gently? The whole family?)

> ✔ As Ian walked unsteadily across the road, he stumbled, and shattered the glass.

> ✔ The whole family will enjoy stuffed peppers simmered gently for half-an-hour.

Myself

Myself can be used correctly as a reflexive pronoun:

> I wash **myself**.

Myself can be used correctly as an emphasising pronoun:

> I saw it **myself**

It cannot be used like this:

> ✗ My husband and **myself** were there.

> ✗ He shook hands with my husband and **myself**.

Use personal pronouns instead:

> ✔ My husband and **I** were there.

> ✔ He shook hands with my husband and with **me**.

There are no such words as theirselves/themselfs!

The pronoun is **themselves** and can be used reflexively or emphatically:

> ✔ They wash **themselves**.

> ✔ They saw it **themselves**.

Negatives

Be careful to avoid an unintentional double negative:

> I do**n't** eat **hardly** any breakfast. = I eat a lot of breakfast.

One

The impersonal pronoun **one** can sound a little pompous and might be best avoided. However, if you do use it, make sure that you 'keep it up' and don't mix it with other pronouns:

> ✗ If **one** uses gloss paint, **you** should clean **your** brushes with white spirit.
>
> ✔ If **one** uses gloss paint, **one** should clean **one's** brushes with white spirit.
>
> ✔ If **you** use gloss paint, **you** should clean **your** brushes with white spirit.

Only

Take great care to position **only** in a sentence beside the word it refers to. It has a very powerful effect on meaning:

> *Only* **my father** eats chips at home. (= nobody else)
>
> My father eats *only* **chips** at home. (= no other food)
>
> My father eats chips *only* **at home**. (= nowhere else)

Prepositions

Use the correct preposition. Your dictionary will guide you:

> to object **to**, to insist **on**, to be antagonistic **towards**

Take great care to select the correct preposition to convey your exact meaning. There is often a range of possible choices but the meaning varies accordingly:

> 'to look **in**' is different from 'to look **into**'
>
> 'to look **over**' is different from 'to look **up**'
>
> 'to look **on**' is different from 'to look **out**'

Don't skimp on prepositions:

> ✗ Meg was prejudiced and hostile **to** all changes.
>
> ✔ Meg was prejudiced **against** and hostile **to** all changes.
>
> ✔ Meg was prejudiced **against** all changes and hostile **to** them.

The sequence of tenses

Tenses divide themselves into four time zones:

- present
- future
- past
- future-in-the-past.

You can use tenses from the first two time zones together in a sentence, and tenses from the last two time zones together. Most of the time, we do this instinctively.

Use any of these tenses together:

Present tenses	**Future tenses**
he hopes	he will meet
he is hoping	he will be meeting
he does hope	he is going to meet
he has hoped	he is about to meet
he has been hoping	he will have met
	he will have been meeting

    ✔ He **hopes** that he **will meet** me in London.

    ✔ He **has been hoping** that he **will have met** me before his parents **arrive**.

Use any of these tenses together:

Past tenses	**Future-in-the-past tenses**
he hoped	he would meet
he was hoping	he would be meeting
he did hope	he would have met
he had hoped	he would have been meeting
he had been hoping	
he used to hope	

    ✔ He **had hoped** that he **would have met** me before his parents **arrived**.

    ✔ He **had been hoping** that he **would meet** me in London.

Don't switch tenses in mid-stream

If you decide to tell a story in the past tense, you must keep to the decision and not wander between the past and the present for no good reason.

Shall/will

The straightforward future tense goes like this:

I **shall** go   we **shall** go
you **will** go (singular)   you **will** go (plural)
he, she, it **will** go   they **will** go

✔ I **shall** go to Portsmouth next week.

If you reverse **shall** and **will**, you introduce a note of determination into the future tense:

✔ I **will** go to the disco! (i.e. whatever you say!)

✔ 'Cinderella, you **shall** go to the ball!'

Should/would

The conditional tense goes like this:

I **should** go   we **should** go
you **would** go   you **would** go
he/she/it **would** go   they **would** go

This is the correct construction to use in a formal letter:

'I **should** be grateful if you **would** send...'

Who/whom at the beginning of questions

_____ is there? (who or whom?)

_____ did you see? (who or whom?)

Pose a possible answer using he/him and the form of the pronoun you want becomes clear:

_____ is there? **He** is there. ➡ **Who** is there?

_____ did you see? I saw **him**. ➡ **Whom** did you see?

Who/whom in the middle of the sentence

The assistant _____ served me had red hair. (who or whom?)

The assistant _____ I thanked had red hair. (who or whom?)

Break the sentence down to two sentences and use he/him as a reference point again:

The assistant had red hair. **He** served me. ➡ The assistant **who** served me had red hair.

The assistant had red hair. I thanked **him**. ➡ The assistant **whom** I thanked had red hair.